Synthetic Real Estate Investment for the Small Investor

First Edition

William S. Mathers

Copyright © 2010 by William S. Mathers

No part of this book can be reproduced by any means without prior permission of the author, except as permitted under Section 107 or 108 of the 1976 United States Copyright Act.

Request for permissions or further information or requests should be directed via Email to: syntheticbookinfo@cfl.rr.com.

Limit of Liability / Disclaimer of Warranty: Even though author has made his best efforts in preparing the book, the author makes no representations or warranties with the respect to the accuracy or completeness of the book and specifically disclaims all warranties, including without limitation warranties of merchantability or fitness for a particular purpose. The advice or strategies contained herein may not be suitable for every situation. You should consult with a professional where appropriate. The author shall not be liable for any loss of profits or any damages, included but not limited to special, incidental, consequential, or other damages.

ISBN 1450547923

To my family and friends.

Table of Contents

Author		ix
Introduction		xi
1.0 Value		3
1.1	Location, location, location.	4
1.1.1	Ricardian Rent	8
1.1.2	Competing Use	12
1.1.3	Future Growth in Location Value	14
1.2	Property Value over Time	16
1.2.1	Herengracht Location Value Index	17
1.2.2	Is a Home a Good Investment?	40
2.0 Cycles		45
2.1	Regions	46
2.1.1	Outputs: Effect on Regional Growth	48
2.1.2	Housing	51
2.1.3	Speculation	56
3.0 Risk vs. Reward		61
3.1	Feasibility	61
3.2	Flipping	67
3.3	Rental Homes	71
3.4	Overview	76
4.0 A Brief History of Derivatives		83
4.1	Ancient History	84
4.2	Medieval Europe	88
4.3	A Major Step Forward	91
4.4	The New World	93
4.5	The Computer Age	94

4.6	Property Derivatives	96
5.0 Real Estate Indices		99
5.1	NPI	100
5.2	Radar Logic's RPX	106
5.3	S&P / Case-Shiller	109
6.0 Property Derivatives		119
6.1	Swaps and Forwards	119
6.2	Real Estate Futures	125
6.3	Options	136
7.0 Synthetic Market Exposure		145
7.1	Synthetic Flipping	146
7.2	Synthetic Rental Property	155
8.0 Hedging		163
8.1	Hedging Real Estate	163
8.1.1	Hedging against increasing value	178
9.0 Portfolio Management		181
9.1	Portfolio Theory	182
9.1.1	Portfolio Allocation	186
9.1.2	Sharpe-Maximizing Portfolio	195
Afterword		203
References		207
Index		210

Author

William Mathers is a real estate developer and professional structural engineer. Over the past several years, he has been involved in numerous projects of different size and type.

His interest in synthetic real estate came about as a direct result of the collapse of the housing market and financial system. As a development partner who had worked for years getting a few large projects pushed through approval, he witnessed the collapse firsthand. Many of the projects he was a partner in would now fail. He had worked for years with nothing to show for it.

With a background conducting forensic investigations, he set about to find out how such devastation could be avoided in the future. Figuring his research would only require a few days, he set about to solve how to control risk in his future real estate projects. One and a half years later, after several dead ends he came across synthetic real estate positions. The markets and mechanisms were already in place. It was a perfect new way to invest and hedge real estate.

Introduction

A synthetic is a replacement for the original. The synthetic mimics the desired properties of the original, but with added advantages. *Synthetic real estate* is a new way for small investors to capitalize on residential real estate investment with the added advantages of less capital and risk. Utilizing property derivatives to synthesize physical real estate, the investor can profit in rising and falling housing markets without having to purchase a physical property. We do not need banks to finance our investments, and we do not need to haggle with property buyers and sellers. All of our transactions can be done electronically with a few clicks of a mouse. *Synthetic Real Estate for the Small Investor* was written to provide the average real estate investor with sufficient background and information to be able to execute synthetic real estate strategies.

The book is broken down into three sections. The first part of the book deals with real property in terms of value. Our goal is not to appraise the value of a single home, but to understand basic macro and micro urban economic theory of what makes regions tick. We explore city evolution to understand why there is a downtown, suburbs, and blight. Next, we look at property values to understand why they vary at different points within the city – how different uses compete for the same location (and who wins). We discover why property values in regions go up and down, and we look at bubbles. Finally, we analyze physical real estate investment to discuss the true risks involved.

In the second part of the book, we learn about derivatives. Far from the monsters that they have been portrayed as, we find derivatives to be a useful tool. In order to have property derivatives, we need a proper index. Each of the major indices is covered for U.S. property derivatives. We learn how each index is computed, and what makes the index value rise and fall. Next, we look at the actual "tools" of synthetic real estate, the property derivatives.

The third part of the book deals with applications and strategies utilizing synthetic real estate. Here we explore putting what we have learned to practice. Strategies and examples of how to take advantage of home price movement are illustrated. If we still make physical real estate investments, we learn how we can now hedge some of our risk. Finally, we look at using real estate to diversify our portfolio of investments.

Part 1

Housing, the Underlying

"An investment in knowledge pays the best interest"

– Ben Franklin

1.0 Value

There are several common expressions in real estate. Location, location, location; home values always go up over time; our home is a good investment. They are some of the most often heard idioms. Most of these expressions have been derived from sound principles that had been noticed over time, however; the expressions are over simplified and need to be investigated further. Location, location, location - why, why, why? Do real estate prices really go up over time? Is this home a good investment or just a money pit?

All of our questions have one thing in common. They address the value of a property, not just in the sense of purchase price, but in consideration of the buyer's intentions. If the property being purchased is a primary residence, the value may be measured in the quality of life. Investors will measure property value in terms of its ability to produce income and a return at sale. Speculators, also known as flippers, look to turn a quick profit by purchasing and selling properties that they consider undervalued.

In the following pages, we will explore value of a home in a broad economic sense. Our focus is to understand the basic principles of why overall home values are at various levels in different regions – not the specific value of a house with x number of bedrooms and a pool. We will strive to develop a basic understanding of what factors affect overall home values so we can make sound investment decisions, and avoid making costly mistakes based on emotions and media "noise".

1.1 Location, location, location.

Also known as the three rules of real estate, the expression cuts to the heart of property investment. Since we cannot move the property, its location is of paramount importance. If we have ever seen a map of a city with real estate values – a topographical map, we would notice that the values tend to peak at the city's center (downtown) then decline as we move away. Granted there are some exceptions or other areas of high value, nonetheless; the overall trend is a high concentration of value that tapers off to the borders. Why do most cities exhibit this behavior? To answer this question we will need to review some economic theory on how cities evolve. The following scenario is a bit oversimplified, but does illustrate how a city evolves – city evolution.

Imagine a town back before automobiles and zoning regulations. Our town is surrounded by flat plains of

1.0 Value

agricultural land – think of a dartboard with the town in the bull's-eye. In town, the crops and livestock are brought to be processed, sold, and exported. Other businesses will soon sprout up to take advantage of the commerce happening in the town. Small shops, bars, and banks locate near the processing centers and markets. In order to operate these facilities and due to transportation constraints workers would naturally choose to have their residences nearby. As time goes by, new industries have opened near processing plants in order to take advantage of being close to their raw products. The industries require new workers who will also require accommodations within a reasonable travel distance to their workplace. Since walking is our main mode of worker transportation, the accommodations will need to be within a reasonable walking distance.

As our town grows, it will need to convert some of the surrounding agricultural land into either residential or commercial uses. However, the conversion of use will not occur unless the value of housing exceeds the value of the agricultural land – the farmer will not sell at a loss. Residential property being developed on the outskirts of town will tend to cost less, since the workers will need to be compensated for having to travel further to work. Now there may be with large estates, but the average house of the day gets cheaper the further away from the city.

Something interesting is about to happen. Because land at the city center is so expensive, it makes more sense to develop multiple units on a single property – apartment buildings. Workers can now opt to live closer to work without having to move farther away from the center of town and work. Office buildings will eventually need to go vertical to rent enough space to be able to justify the land purchase price. Our town becomes a city - growing in land area and density.

Fast forward a few decades, and introduce the automobile and highways. With the improved transportation, the physical proximity to employment is not as important. It is all about the commute time. The utility of the older houses is seen as inadequate by most our population. Everyone wants a driveway, garage, yard, and more than one bathroom, "the American Dream". Developers find that the value of agricultural land is less than developed residential lots, and subdivisions are born. With a short commute from downtown, the middle class worker leaves the city center for the new subdivisions. The suburbs are born.

Downtown, the apartments are under pressure – they are losing the middle class families to the suburbs. People who can afford housing do not wish to live close to industry. Therefore, the apartment owners are left renting housing to workers who cannot afford or make enough income to move. The areas around industry will deteriorate as less is spent to maintain buildings in order to offset lost income.

Fast forward again, and we now find our city is a commuter city. The downtown is full of office buildings, but nobody lives there. Workers drive into work in the morning and leave in the afternoon. At night, the downtown for all intensive purposes is a ghost town. Blighted communities surround the downtown and are where most of the industrial plants are located (if they remain in business). Developers have supplied lots in subdivisions further out from the city center, but the traffic jams and high commute times have put a limit on how far they can go. Our agriculturally based town is now a service and manufacturing hub. The city's economy no longer depends on agriculture. What happened to most our farmers? Well, many became developers as the value of their land for residential use exceeded the value for agriculture. Seems like we have reached our growth limit, the streets and highways are jammed.

Luckily, we have developers willing to solve our problems. Anticipating that commercial uses would produce more value than residential, the development of office and other commercial spaces has begun in the suburbs. Our suburbanites will now have the option of much shorter commutes to work and shopping. With agricultural land around the suburb being cheap, new residential development will begin to radiate out from the new commercial hubs – pending growth of business and population. Therefore, the cycle begins again. Starting from the center of our dartboard, development has spread out to resemble pepperoni on a pizza.

1.1.1 Ricardian Rent

Again, the evolution of our little town to a large metropolis has been over simplified, but it sets the stage to discuss a principle of urban economics, Ricardian rent. David Ricardo developed the theory back in 1817 to try to explain why the value of homes, or rent in his case, varies across a city. The theory is idealized, but we get a good understanding of the basic economics of property value. The main assumption we will begin with is that property owners will rent their land to those willing to pay the most. Next, we assume that the city and urban area is round with our downtown in the center where everybody works – back to our dartboard. All of our workers commute directly to work with a cost of x per mile, but they are each located at various distances d (in miles) from the city center. All households are the same size with an income that can be spent on housing, commuting, and other goods. The households live in the same type of house that cost the same to build with the same density. The only difference between our households is the distance to work.

If everything were the same, why would rents vary across the city? Well, it works out this way – remember the cost of commuting is x per mile. Since all incomes are fixed, a worker who lives farther away from the city center will have to pay more for the commute. The income they can spend on housing and other goods is reduced with each additional mile away from the city center. As all of the houses cost the same to build, the portion of rent the

1.0 Value

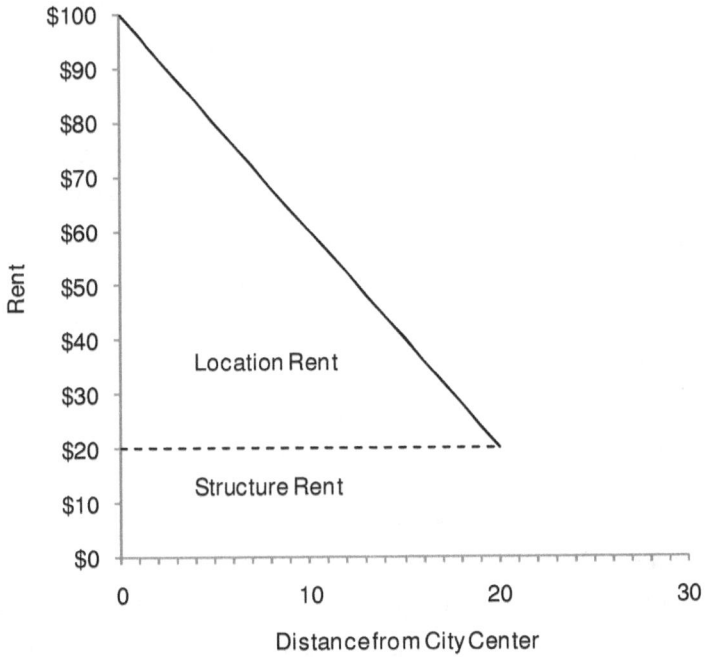

Figure 1.1-A, Residential Rent Curve

property owner needs to attribute to the physical structure is the same across the whole city – structure rent. Because each worker will want to maximize the amount of income to spend on other goods beside commuting and housing, we find that the location value – location rent – is reduced as we move away from the city center. With each additional mile of distance, the land rent will reduce at the rate of the cost of commuting (See Figure 1.1-A). Therefore, at the center of the city the commute cost is zero allowing the highest rents to be charged. At the perimeter of the city where the commute cost is the highest, the location rent would be zero. Rent at the outskirts would only need to cover the cost of the house as the land has little location rent value.

Logically the model makes sense. Each worker would like to maximize the amount of income they could spend on other items besides commuting and housing. Competition for rental units would cause housing to fill up, which would require workers to move further away. In order to compensate for higher commuting costs, property owners would need to have lower rents. Our rental model is almost complete, but we need to consider one more item.

Let us look again at our rental values at the city's perimeter. We said the land was worthless, but this was an oversimplification. At the perimeter of development, the land is usually agricultural land that has value based on the crop production. The owner of the property would be able to charge the farmer rental fees for the use of the property know as agricultural rent. Going back to our house at the edge of the city, we see the rent is composed of three parts; location rent (zero at the city's perimeter); structural rent, and agricultural rent (See Figure 1.1-B).

Now that we have all three pieces of the model, we see that agricultural rent is constant across all property. If the land were more valuable as a farm – it would remain so. The model is idealized so structural rent, the cost to cover the building itself, is also constant across all property. The only component of the rent that changes is the location rent. As we go from the outskirts to the city center, the location rent increases at the rate of decreasing commuter costs.

Figure 1.1-B, Residential rent curve with agricultural rent.

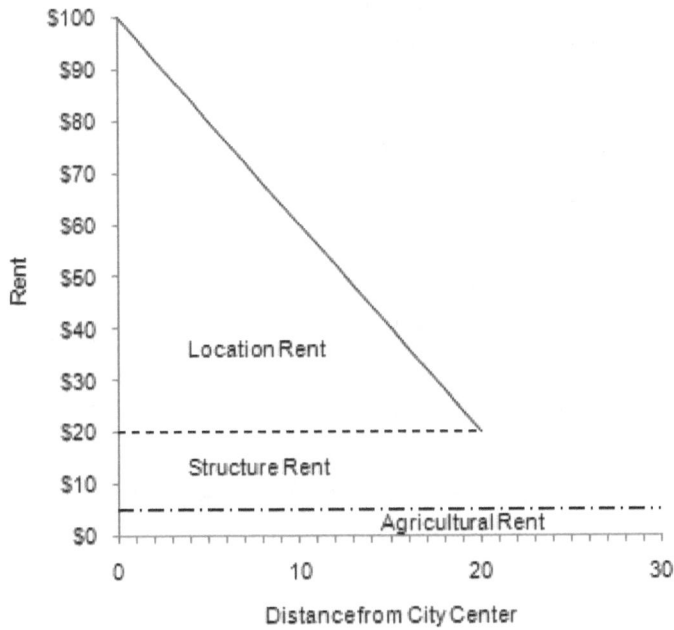

1.1.2 Competing Uses

To add another layer of reality and complexity, let us consider that there are two household types competing to rent homes. All other factors will remain the same except household "A" really hates to commute. They do not mind spending more income for rent as long as they do not have to commute far. Household "B" does not mind commuting. For simplicity let us set the cost of commuting for household "A" at twice the cost of household "B". Here we are relating everything back to dollars and cents, but in real life, the value of the commuting time may be measured in different ways by different people. Household "A" workers value the additional free time more than the additional cost of rent – figure they are willing to pay 30% more in rent for time. What does our city landscape look like? Look at Figure 1.1-C.

Well, our property owners only take the highest offered rent, so at the city center the housing would be dominated by household "A" renters. Household "A" would dominate the rental market until their commuting cost has reduced the rent they were willing to pay away from the city center matched household "B"'s value. At this slope intercept point, we would find a mix of households. Moving further away from the city, and because the slope of commuting costs is less, we would find only household "B" renters.

1.0 Value

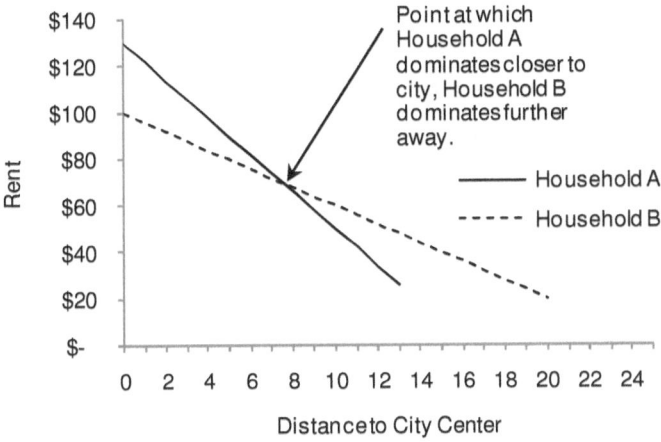

Figure 1.1-C, Rent curve with competing uses.

If we were to try to develop a more realistic model, we could introduce competing industries along with our households. Each industry would have a different commute cost, however their commuting cost would relate more toward their industry. For instance, a shipping company may have very little commuting costs. Lower commuting costs would locate them out toward the edge of the city, perhaps beyond our housing. Commercial office space may need to be near the city center, and in order to get the location they will pay much higher rents than homeowners will. With a high commuting costs (a need to be near the downtown) and ability to pay higher rent, owners of property will favor commercial property over housing near the city center – and so on. The property will eventually find its highest and best use. As we add complexity with additional industries, and perhaps a few extra households, the model begins to resemble a real city. If we took a chart of rental values from the center of the center to the outskirts, we would see the result of all our industries and housing types form a curve – the bid rent curve.

How does all this modeling of rent translate into value? This is a bit more complicated and abstract, but does relate directly. The price of housing, or any property, is the present discounted value of the rental income stream that is composed of agricultural value, structure value, location value, and newly added future growth in location value. To convert the rental rate into value we merely divide each rent component by the discount rate. The discount rate could be the interest rate, an investment hurdle rate, or derived through complex modeling. We will skip over the complex mathematics and focus on our new term, future growth in location value.

1.1.3 Future Growth in Location Value

As a city's population grows, the perimeter also expands. At the perimeter, agricultural land is being converted to residential or commercial property. The conversion of land usage is where the largest increase in property value occurs since little or no premium is being paid for location. The entire rental income or purchase price only needs to cover structural and agricultural values. As we look inward toward the city center, property values will rise with growth but at a reduced rate since we must now consider location value. There may be as much as 4% difference between the

1.0 Value

city center and perimeter growth rates. What happens beyond our city's border? At the fringe of development, the property values will vary based on the future expectations of growth. With a high expectation of growth, usually as the highways are being built, the agricultural land will also acquire a growth premium. Far away from the city center and beyond the border, there may be little or no growth premium, only agricultural value.

Over time, a city's growth will fluctuate. Some cities will cease to grow while others continue. It is the expectation of growth in the city that will affect property values the most. This concept is so important that we will elaborate on it. If two cities are identical in size, the city with the highest prospects for future growth will have higher property values: even if rents in both cities are the same.

Another major contributor to value, which has not been covered, is governmental land use regulation. Local regulators may impose regulations that can be either positive or negative toward values. Sizes of housing units and density requirements are controlled by the municipalities. Even architectural design can be regulated. Impact of local government should be considered when considering where to invest.

1.2 Property Value over Time

We have had a good discussion on how a city could evolve along with an economic model to rationalize the process. Our models and discussions assumed that growth was constant. Oversimplified? Yes, but we needed to get ourselves introduced to some basic theory. Now with a basic understanding of urban economics, we will explore the value of housing over time.

Just after construction, structure value makes up the bulk of the property value. Over time, the building will age and loose value – it will depreciate. As time goes on, the building will require continued maintenance to keep its structure value from falling significantly. Location value may steadily increase, but the depreciation of the building can cause the overall property value to decline. Typically, only when significant renovation and improvements are made to the structure is there a jump in total property value. So the value of a property does not increase steadily in a constant linear fashion, it increases in jumps after additional capital has been spent on improvements. It could be argued that the jump in property value is merely the cost of the improvements – if not a little less. At a future point in time, the structure may be considered economically obsolete and will be demolished. Perhaps a better and higher use for the property was found, or the structure had become functionally obsolete. We find that the property value is ultimately limited by the location value. This finding is backed up in the landmark research done by

Eichholtz and Geltner in their paper *"Four Centuries of Location Value: Implications for Real Estate Capital Gain in Central Places"* or *"Four centuries of location value"*.

1.3 Herengracht Location Value Index

Eichholtz and Geltner's paper focused on the Herengracht region just outside the city center in historic Amsterdam. The region made a great location study because initially it was just outside the medieval boundaries of the city. As time passed, the area was eventually incorporated into the downtown commercial district. How much time did they have data for? Try 347 years worth of data. From 1628 through 1974 they were able to develop an index know as the Herengracht Location Value Index from over 3,851 repeat sale transaction pairs (See Figure 1.3-A). Transaction pairs are the price at which the same house sells over time. Herengracht is also unique in that the address has always been desirable. Incredibly, the buildings remain fairly well intact with modifications to the existing structures being done to keep them from being obsolete. There is virtually no structural depreciation. Therefore, what they were left with was a location value index with the span of three and a half centuries. Another wonderful thing our researchers did was to convert all of the values into an index that could be compared across time to see how location value behaves. The index was divided into nine periods that best explained index levels, and specific periods of history for the Netherlands that have a specific impact on Amsterdam.

Before we delve into our historic timeline, we need to set the stage with a bit of history to understand how our first period came about. At the beginning of the 16th century, Amsterdam was a small port town that was part of seventeen loosely united feudal provinces known as the Habsburg Netherlands. They were ruled over by Emperor

Figure 1.3-A, Herengracht Location Value Index (1628-1974). Source *"Four Centuries of Location Value: Implications for Real Estate Capital Gain in Central Places"* **by Eichholtz and Geltner**

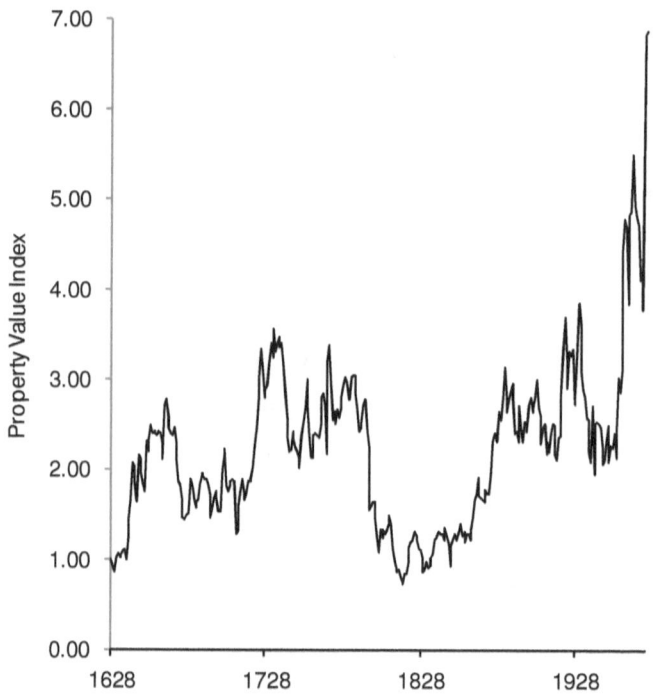

Charles V of Spain. Charles had a fondness for the region since he had been raised there. In 1548, Charles granted the seventeen provinces limited autonomy and made it a separate territory from either Spain or France. Eight years later, Charles abdicated the thrown to his son Philip. Being raised in Spain, Philip did not have the same affinity for the region as his father. Under his father, the region had a bit of autonomy, but Philip wanted direct control over everything. Additionally, his hatred of the Protestant movement caused him to start what was a mini-Inquisition in the region. It was a capital punishment not to be Catholic, and many citizens were killed. All hell broke loose. At first the rebellion was Protestant's defending their rights (and lives), but as the revolt dragged on, Spain was having trouble financing the campaign and occupation – this and other conflicts were draining the treasury. Therefore, they decided to place additional taxes on the local citizens to pay for the conflict. At this point, the Catholic inhabitants, who were oblivious to their fellow Protestant's plight, had enough. The whole region revolted to begin the 80 Years War around 1568.

Through several years of turmoil and atrocities, the territory was divided. Most of the region had been recaptured in the east and south. The new "borders" roughly resemble the modern day borders of the Netherlands on the northwest, with the occupied regions to the south and west being Belgium and Luxemburg. Protestants the occupied Spanish regions were given two years to leave the Habsburg lands or convert. Most chose to leave. Many of those being exiled were highly skilled craftsman and rich merchants from large port cities. They headed north to the self-proclaimed Republic of the Seven United Netherlands – better known as the Dutch Republic. These wealthy and skilled immigrants would have a profound effect on the Dutch Republic, and Amsterdam in particular.

Early 1600, it is the beginning of the Golden Age. In 1609, the Twelve Year's Truce is signed between Spain and the Dutch Republic. The Dutch Republic is officially recognized as a sovereign nation by European countries, and they begin to build a network of consulates. Amsterdam is now becoming one of the most important ports in the world. Windmills have been developed, along with the ability to use peat for fuel. Sawmills are developed which allowed the construction of vast fleets. The Dutch East India Company was formed, and financed through the selling of shares at one of the world's first stock exchanges located in Amsterdam. Merchant banking develops in the region, and insurance was developed. The Dutch economy has become truly modern. In this early period, the country was undergoing industrialization. Worker productivity became the highest in the world. Only 40% of the workforce was needed for agriculture, which not only provided sufficient food for the population, but enough food was produced to be available for export at a profit. As profits from the many industries and trading accumulated,

1.0 Value

there was demand for investing in other opportunities, and again, the Amsterdam stock market would be the place to match the demand and supply of investment funds. In 1620, the Dutch West India Company was formed with a trade monopoly in the Caribbean. With all this economic activity, many other citizens from Germany and the nearby countryside began to migrate to Amsterdam. Immigrants felt that there would always be work in Amsterdam. The city's population grew rapidly.

Figure 1.3-B, Cornelis Anthonisz's *Bird's eye view of Amsterdam,* **1544. Woodcut. Rijksmuseum Amsterdam. Source, Wikimedia**

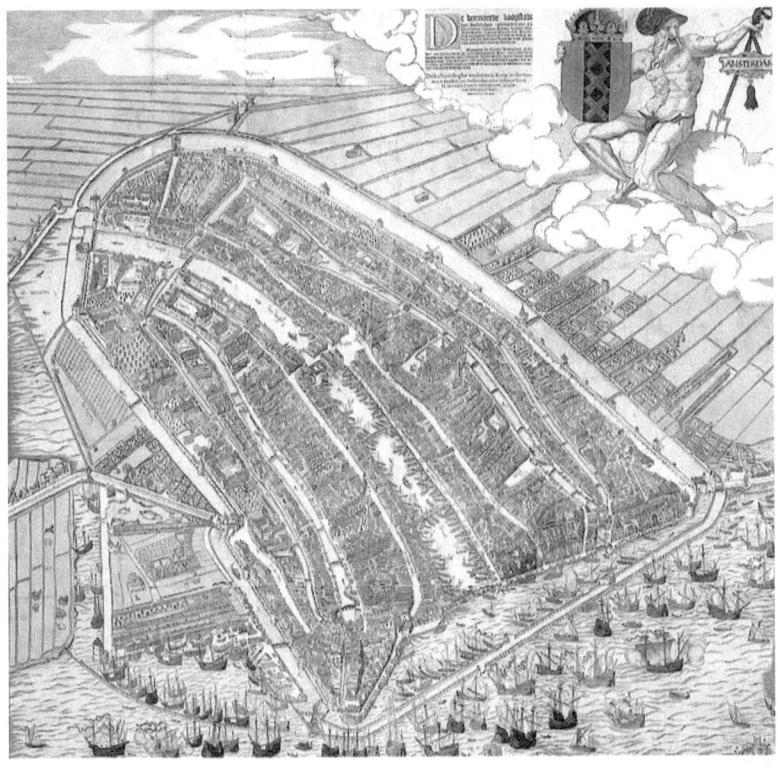

Synthetic Real Estate Investment

The canal system in Amsterdam began construction around 1613. Four canals were to be built around the city's land perimeter – Amsterdam is a port on the coast. The final la wet of the cannels would form semi-circles around the city that start at the bay on the north and end at the bay on the south side of the city. The inner three canals were to be installed for residential development – the Herengracht, the Keizersgracht, and the Prisengracht. An outer canal was to be installed for drainage and defense. The canals were built in two phases. The first phase was the north half of the canals which was completed around 1624. The second phase of construction did not begin until 1664. The canal construction would not be complete until sometime in the late 1600's to early 1700's.

1.3.1.1 First Period (1628-1688)

The Herengracht index is set at 1.0 starting in 1628. The Herengracht region has just been completed four years earlier, and it is located just outside the medieval city boundaries on the north side. The Twelve Year Truce has ended and hostilities between Spain and the Dutch Republic are resuming. During the truce, the Dutch Republic has trained an army that is able to thwart any Spanish invasion plans, and their naval fleet is world class in size and technology. Under the new King of Spain, Philip III, Spain begins waging an economic war with limited military engagements. Further adding to Dutch misfortune, due to the success of their traders, other countries such as England and France enact protectionist measures such as tariffs to help their fellow citizens compete. Trading profits are stagnant, so investment capital moves from trading ventures to infrastructure projects, such as building the dike system to convert lakes into useable land. There is some growth in Amsterdam, but as the index shows property values in our region is flat and unchanged until 1638. Spain's economic stranglehold is effective along with the trade tariffs.

Around 1625, England enters the war alongside the Dutch. The war has gone from an economic war to an all out shooting war, but with England entering the battle, the tide begins to turn against the Spanish. The Spanish end their

1.3-C, Herengracht Index (1628-1688), Source *"Four Centuries of Location Value: Implications for Real Estate Capital Gain in Central Places"* **by Eichholtz and Geltner**

blockades in 1629. Other regional wars end, which further open up trade routes that had been constricted. France enters an alliance with the Dutch Republic against Spain in 1635. Soon, Germany begins ordering food and weapons from Dutch suppliers for its military ambitions. Incomes soar, and residential real estate values double, the index rises over the next ten years from around 1.0 to 2.0 for location value. Finally, in 1648, there is peace between Spain and the Republic – France would continue fighting Spain for another ten years. For now the Dutch can get back to business, the Spanish embargo is over.

The industrious Republic is now humming. For the next twenty years, the country will experience prosperity. They will rise to be the world leader in trade with only one conflict, the First Anglo-Dutch War (1652-1654). With incomes and profits up again, we see that real estate values will also increase. The Herengracht index will climb from 2.0 in 1648 to 2.5 in 1668. During this growth period, there is one significant dip in values in 1662, which corresponds with an outbreak of bubonic plague.

Bubonic plague is spread by fleas that are found on rats and mice. Since Amsterdam received products from all over the globe, they are highly susceptible to the spread of epidemics. Rats and mice easily stow away on ships that provide a convenient way for viruses to hop from one continent to the next. This plague outbreak is believed to have originated from Algiers on the content of Africa. Because of the plague, ships were quarantined for thirty

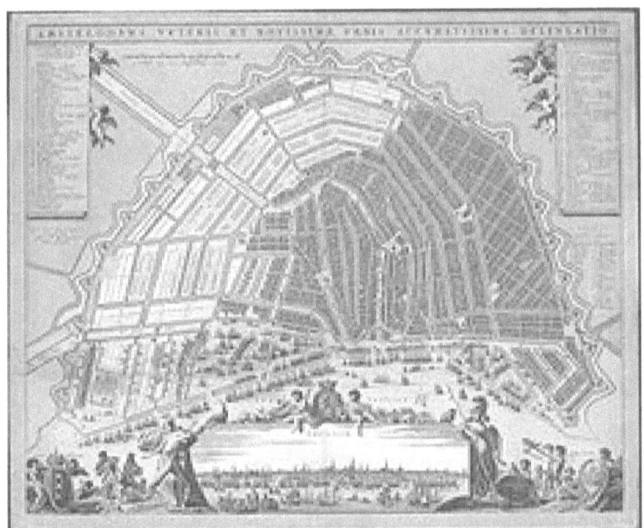

Figure 1.3-D, Map of Amsterdam in 1662 by Daniel Stalpaert. Photographed by Nicolaus Visscher. Source, Wikimedia

days before being allowed to unload their cargo. Nearly 10% of the population of Amsterdam died during this epidemic. Rich residents left the city for the countryside in search of safety. A local sentiment arose that the canals had something to do with the spread of the disease. Property values on the canals such as the Herengracht suffered. The plague seems to have diminished by 1665, and once again, Amsterdam got back to business.

1672 is known as the Disastrous Year. The Dutch would face two major challenges. First, war had been declared against the Republic by England, France, Münster, and Cologne. This war was started over the French Kings anger that the Dutch Republic did not assist him a few years earlier in invading the lower provinces currently known as the Spanish Netherlands. As always, these wars expanded to include many nations taking sides. In an interesting twist, Spain would join the Dutch. England and France invaded the Dutch Republic, but were repelled at a high cost. Friendly German principalities assisted the Dutch in holding off Münster and Cologne, however; territory was lost. Peace was brokered with England in 1674, but it would not be until 1679 when France (and by this time a whole host of other nations) would finalize a truce.

The war cut trade off with almost all of markets the Dutch traded, and the prices of many exports began to decline. Other regions with lower waged workers began to industrialize and provide the same products at lower costs, outsourcing. To counter, the manufacturers in Amsterdam switched to producing higher-end products, but without much avail. Incomes declined. Furthermore, many investments were not doing very well. The Dutch West India Company went bust in 1674 due to excessive debt and rivalry with the English – a second company would be started. The Dutch East India Company also had issues. Due to political issues they had to change from trading high profit goods to low profit bulk goods, such as tea and pepper. To make matters worse, they now had to compete with other companies – specifically the British East India Company. A price war ensued, and although the Dutch East India Company actually expanded, there was no growth in profits. It was a profitless growth.

The war and economic issues dealt a severe blow to the Dutch Republic – The Golden Age had ended. Back in the Herengracht region of Amsterdam, we see that property values plummeted. In 1671, the index was at 2.12. During the war, the index fell as low as 1.45 and settled at 1.51 as the war was beginning to wind down in 1678. Almost 38 years of property value gains had been lost. It would be fifty years until property values would reach levels equal to the 1660's. For the next seven years (1678-1685), there was growth in Amsterdam property values. The Herengracht Index hops around a bit with some volatility. We do not exit this period of study without more intrigue. These next events will set of a chain reaction that will affect our property values for the next fifty years.

Louis XIV of France had aims of expanding his empire. Following the end of the war, he set up the Chambers of Reunion to make sure France received all of the territories it was owed based on the various treaties from recent and not-so recent conflicts. The claims were based on archaic medieval laws, which as one would expect, favored his claims and land grabs. In fact, they even made some stuff up and took territories from countries who were too preoccupied with other conflicts to do anything about it. Things were getting a bit out of hand when in 1683 Spain was forced into war. They had found French forces were beginning to occupy some of their territories, such as the Spanish Netherlands. The war was short, but brutal and ended in 1684. To make matters worse, King Louis XIV in

1685 revoked the Edict of Nantes, which granted French Protestants basic rights as citizens since 1598 – now they would be treated as heretics. Protestant churches were ordered to be destroyed and Protestant schools closed. Hundreds of thousands of French Protestants would leave France over the next twenty years for England, the Dutch Republic, and other more tolerant regions. As one would expect, France was becoming very unpopular around Europe. Once again, a significant portion of the refuges would be highly skilled workers who probably helped provide for the rise in Herengracht property values due to population growth of Amsterdam.

Across the way, England was beginning to experience its own internal turmoil in regards to religion. In 1673 and 1678, Charles II had passed legislative Acts that required anyone holding a public office, such as serving in Parliament, or holding a government job had to be a member in the Anglican Church of England – the established church for the country. On his deathbed, Charles II converted to Catholicism and appointed his brother James II to the thrown – Charles had no legitimate children. James was a Catholic and his assumption of the throne was not popular. Things were going to get worse. James wanted to repeal the Acts that punished Catholics. When Parliament disagreed – he shut them down. He was a bit of an absolutist. He replaced various high offices with Catholic favorites, employed a standing army, and put Catholic officers in charge. Now the country tolerated him feeling his reign was an anomaly, and his daughters were Protestant – so, it would all eventually pass. Until, his wife bore a son in 1688. Now fears of a Catholic dynasty in England would push events forward.

How does this tie into the Dutch Republic? Well, it just so happens that a regional governor in Holland, William III was a prince by birth. He was also married to James II's daughter Mary. In addition, he was known in England and a Protestant. He had been caught up in the turmoil in England, and had ambitions of profiting from his marriage to Mary. When James's wife had produced a male heir, several noble men invited him come over and "save the Protestant religion". Agents were sent out to spread propaganda in favor of his taking the throne of England. He felt he required a large invasion force, so he asked his current compatriots, the Dutch Republic to assist.

At first, the Dutch were reluctant, knowing firsthand the enormous cost of war, and felt this was unnecessary. However, in 1687, King Louis XIV of France tried to intimidate the Dutch by imposing large trade tariffs and seizing all Dutch ships that were in French ports. This was to serve as a warning for the Dutch to stay clear of this matter. However, William and supporters were able to spin it as France's imminent desire to invade the Republic. Since they had just recently fought off both England and France, they were persuaded that by helping William they would not suffer another Anglo-French attack. This would be a pre-emptive operation for self-defense. Alliances were entered into with other nations, specifically with the motivation of joining against France. Even the Holy Roman Empire sided with William when he agreed not to persecute Catholics in England. A Grand Alliance is formed in Europe.

The Dutch Republic invades England in 1688, sparking off the "Glorious Revolution". With no major conflicts, William and his wife Mary were established as joint monarchs of England by 1689. James fled to his cousin and alley, Louis XIV of France.

We are at the end of the first period. Our index has finished at a value of 1.94, and with a local in charge of one of the world's current super powers, the local's must be feeling good about the future. If only life could be as simple to allow us to use the fairy tale ending: "and they lived happily ever after".

1.3.1.2 Second Period (1689-1789)

We begin the period with a location value in the Herengracht region of 1.89. The boundaries of the city of Amsterdam have grown to the south, but the location of the Herengracht region in relation to the city's center (proximity to its downtown / commercial areas) has remained relatively unchanged. Remarkably, this will be the case for the next 100 years.

1.0 Value

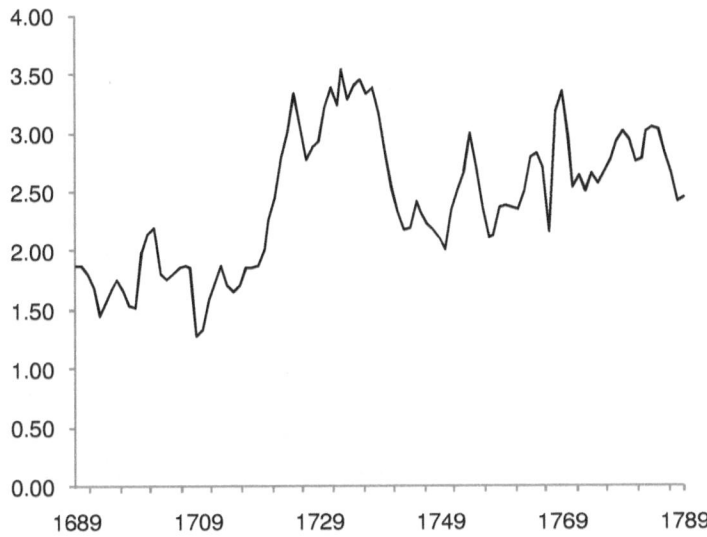

Figure 1.3-E, Herengracht Index (1689-1789), Source *"Four Centuries of Location Value: Implications for Real Estate Capital Gain in Central Places"* **by Eichholtz and Geltner**

Williams' success in England began the Nine Years War where he commanded both the English and Dutch forces. The war started in Ireland and spread throughout Europe and the colonies. By 1697, the war ended with France being the ultimate victor in preserving many of the land grabs it had taken earlier. However, there was a new controversy brewing as territories were being shuffled about. The succession of the Spanish thrown was becoming an issue, as it could unite Spain and France into a superpower. All involved were attempting to keep a balance of power in the region.

The King of Spain, Charles II died in 1700 leaving his kingdom to his half-sisters grandson Philip, who also happened to be grandson to our friend King Louis XIV of France. Philip was announced as King over all the former Spanish territories, which violated treaties from the Nine Years War. During the war, those territories had been effectively lost. Louis wanted to cement his grandsons hold and the potential for French dominance. He had made several tactical moves, which strained relationships with England. The final straw was when France recognized James II son as the rightful monarch of England. The War of the Spanish Succession would begin in 1701, and last past William III's death until 1714. The Dutch were dragged into the war. Fighting would be all over Europe to include the lands of the Dutch Republic. At the end of the war, the Dutch amassed a huge debt. England would gain the most with new territories in the Americas; the Dutch would receive some forts in the Spanish Netherlands and the territory adjacent to it – Guelders.

With most of the country's attentions toward warfare, there was not much growth of any kind. From 1689 through the end of the wars in 1714, the property location values back in Herengracht remain relatively flat. There was a quick jump up after the Nine Years War ended, but those values would again plummet with the start of the War of the Spanish Succession. Wars had disrupted profitable trade and commerce, and had placed an enormous debt on the country.

During the remainder of the period, the Republic would undergo considerable economic changes – there would be a shift from industry to service sectors. After 1719, the Dutch maintained a policy of neutrality except when their treaties with the English required them to send troops to fight in Ireland in 1745. Besides that - they were neutral and under the protection of the British Admiralty. Dutch ships went from trading only local goods to shipping companies that shipped for merchants in other parts of the world. Due to high wages and taxation, most of the industrial and agricultural production also shifted more to higher-end products (again) to compete on quality as compared to quantity. Much of the industrial plants would end up in England, financed with Dutch investment looking to capitalize on lower wages. With exports, they now had to compete with other burgeoning trading posts such as Hamburg, Bremen, and London. One bright spot is that the Amsterdam, along with London, was the central markets in Europe. Over time, however, London would eventually take the lead.

The period after the war had very little growth in terms of population for Amsterdam. In fact, the researchers describe this period as stagnant. After the wars, property values do seem to rest at a new index level of above 2.0 – so location values were up over the earlier part of the period. Levels did not increase as much as the Golden Age when the country was developing, but did increase until the fatal year of 1780.

1.3.1.3 Third Period: End of the Republic (1790-1850)

1776 – The American colonies declare their independence and form the United States of America. Since the beginning of the American Revolution in 1775, merchants in Amsterdam had been providing the rebels with arms and munitions in exchange for tobacco and indigo. Around 1778, Spain and France entered the War of the American Revolution. England tried to pressure the Dutch Republic to side with them against France, but they refused – preferring to export supplies to France. Adding insult to injury, the Dutch ships were using their neutral status to send arms and supplies to England's enemies. Relations worsened to a boiling point, when in 1780 England declared war on the Dutch Republic to begin the Fourth Anglo-Dutch War.

Since 1719, the Dutch had relied on other countries – predominately England – to provide military protection and support. Therefore, the English were easily able to defeat their Dutch adversaries. By 1784, the Dutch surrendered. Blaming the current government, internal turmoil eventually led to revolt. By 1795, the Dutch Republic is overthrown, and the Batavian Republic is formed, with the backing of the French Republic. The new republic would only last a few years. Napoleon took over France around 1800, and proclaimed himself Emperor in 1804. English embargoes and Napoleons trade policies ground the Dutch trading economy to a halt. The population of Amsterdam

1.0 Value

declined. Eventually the entire country was annexed into Imperial France in 1810.

Looking at the index, we see a catastrophe in land value. As population and incomes fell, so did our index. At the beginning of the period in 1791, we were at a value of 2.7. Within the next 24-years, the index would drop to 0.75. In 1815, property values were technically lower than at any time in the history of Amsterdam. We would not see a real growth in property location values until 1851.

Figure 1.3-F, Herengracht Index (1790-1850), Source *"Four Centuries of Location Value: Implications for Real Estate Capital Gain in Central Places"* **by Eichholtz and Geltner**

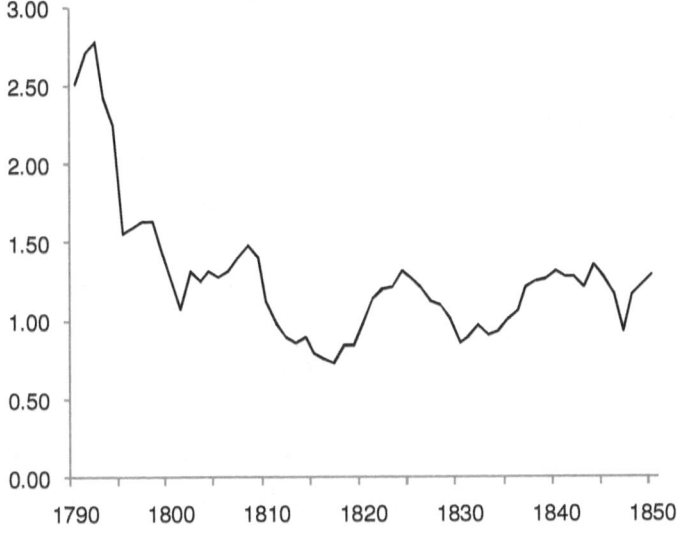

1.3.1.4 Periods Four to Nine (1851-1974)

Not to say that the following periods are any less important, but the magnitude of events are spread out over the next five periods of the study. I hope that we can now appreciate how external events can have a profound effect on the location value. In this next section, we will wrap up the next 123 years in the index and highlight specific valuation impacts as put forth by Eichholtz and Geltner. It is time to put on our seatbelts...

1851-1880. Industrialization finally comes to the Netherlands. With new technologies come new jobs resulting in an increase in population in Amsterdam. During this period, transportation is still limited so the population increase results in increased density – not so much an expansion of the city border. Therefore, location values rise from 1.2 at the beginning of the period to 2.5 in 1880.

1880-1913, the population of Amsterdam nearly doubles, industrialization continues to increase productivity, and personal income continues to rise; however, our value index is flat across the period. We begin with an index value of 2.5 and end with an index value of 2.5. How could this be? When cities grow the property's location value is supposed to increase. Technically, the location value did increase. The cost of commuting changed thanks to a newly developed public transportation system, the horse tram that appeared around 1875. By 1900, the system was switching

1.0 Value

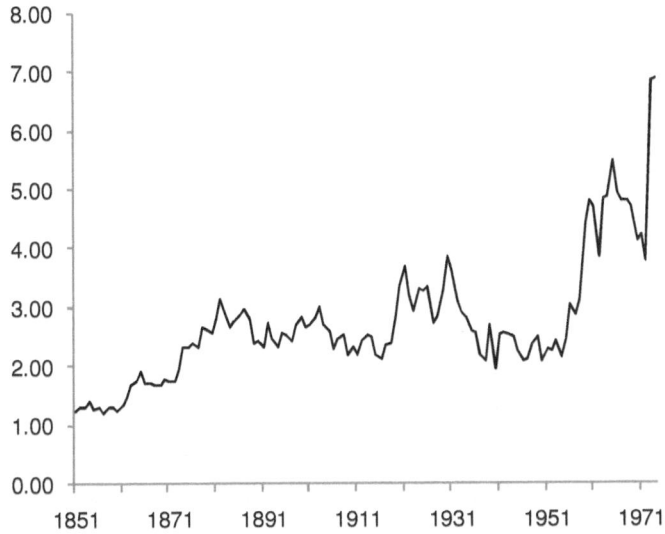

Figure 1.3-G, Herengracht Index (1851-1974), Source *"Four Centuries of Location Value: Implications for Real Estate Capital Gain in Central Places"* **by Eichholtz and Geltner**

over to electric cars and the conversion was 90% complete by 1904. With mass transportation, it was easier for the population to move further out from the city center without a huge effect on the commuter time. As development moved to the peripheries of the city and expanded the boundaries outward, the Herengracht region began to be closer to the city center. However, the technological impact of the trams on commuting costs had the effect of keeping location values unchanged.

1914-1930, the Netherlands had remained neutral during WWI, which helped them avoid large war debt, damage, and population loss. Their problems began to occur after the war. Germany was a main trading partner, and the chaos in the country following the war caused an economic crisis. Furthermore, world trade did not pick up. Since almost 30% of the economy was dependent on exports, and trading opportunities were limited – the economy suffered. The Netherlands would not see the roaring twenties as in the United States.

In Amsterdam, we find steady growth after the First World War, but the city size did not expand as much. The Herengracht region is now located at the edge of the city's center – downtown is also growing. Location values have jumped up to 4.0, even though the economy and incomes are down. Many of the residences are being converted from residential uses to commercial.

1931-1946: The Great Depression and WWII. The Netherlands fell into the Great Depression around 1931 with mass unemployment. As fears of war began to grow due to Nazi aggression, the Dutch began to rearm which was responsible for an artificial recovery in 1938. In the summer of 1940, Germany invaded and occupied the country until the end of the war – spring 1945. At the beginning of the period, the location value was 4.0, after the war the index fell to 2.0.

1946-1974: Recovery and growth. After the war, there were still many trials and tribulations, but overall it was a growth period for the city and the country. Amsterdam's population grew moderately, while incomes grew significantly. New transportation systems are developed and the automobile gains wide use. The city border expands dramatically – the Herengracht is now a predominately a downtown commercial district with index values at 6.9. Our 347-year odyssey is now at an end.

In summary of the 347-year history, our researchers reached the following conclusions. Over time, there is not much growth in the location value. The average growth rate over the entire timeline was only 0.56% per year. Most of the growth was attributed to the Golden Age in the 1600's and the period 1946-1974. The major increase in location value during the 1600's was due to the Herengracht region going from agricultural land to residential, whilst the major increase in 1946-1974 was the conversion of residential use to commercial use. The other important factor for property values is income growth, which was high during both periods cited.

Stepping a bit away from the researcher's findings, we can take a closer look at the index values. Since we probably will not have 347 years to invest, my concerns are with smaller periods. Even during the worst of times – during the French and Nazi Occupations, there was some price movement each year. Although the average growth rate was only 0.56% per year, the standard deviation (or volatility) of the index is 9.96% over the whole time range. In the 1946-1974 periods, the location value index had a volatility of around 14%; stocks have volatility around 15%. What does this mean? Although the location value itself may average out to a low growth rate over the long haul, we can see that there are periods where the index does move significantly. Furthermore, we can see that there are always periods where values are jumping around – property values are volatile. Therefore, to answer our original question, "do property values go up over time", we would have to conclude – *maybe*.

1.3.2 Is a Home a Good Investment?

Is a home an investment? Yes, we will invest a significant portion of our money and time. Is it a good investment? Depends, the question is equivalent to asking if a particular stock is a good investment. As we have learned there is much more to consider than just a nice neighborhood. Consideration would need to be given to the economy of the nation, and the impacts on the local economy for the period we plan to hold the investment – this would be considered market risk. Next, we would need to determine the specific location and type of home that would make the highest return – let us categorize this as asset risk. Finally, the property will need to be maintained with periodic upgrades – managerial risk.

Asset and managerial risk can be controlled through experience. As we look for a home, we can leverage the experience of others in helping us make a reasonably good decision. With some research most folks would come to realize that many renovations are not needed – again, a bit of experience and help from others. Most importantly, we can also make a decision on how much we plan to spend, our exposure – although there are major faults with our logic that will be covered in a later section. Overall, with a bit of legwork and help from knowledgeable (and honest) professionals we can get a property with a good chance at future value growth.

Market risk is where we run into problems. As we saw in the Herengracht Index, values are highly sensitive to outside events that we generally have no control over. A disease could break out and kill millions causing an exodus from our location, a major industry could be outsourced and cause a decline in population, and home values could plummet. On the positive side, a new industry could evolve causing home values to skyrocket, such as Silicon Valley. For every increase in property values, there is a decrease. What goes up must come down. It really becomes a matter of what degree those movements take, and where the market was when we purchased. If we bought at the high point of a bubble, it may be a very long time before we see values up again. Later on, we will learn how we can hedge market risk, but for most folks purchasing a home they will be fully exposed.

Therefore, in terms of a home, our primary residence, it may be best to consider it a cost of living. Whether we rent or own, there is a cost associated with it. If we are honest about what we truly need and drop the "Mc mansion" fantasy chances are, we will get the most out of our home.

Synthetic Real Estate Investment

A home will give us a good feeling of ownership, and hopefully many happy memories.

For speculators and investors there is plenty of money to be made in residential real estate, but for most people these activities are better left outside our primary residence. When dealing with our primary residence we tend to confuse what we want verses what the market will actually pay for it. Emotions cloud rational decision-making. Ranchers do not raise cattle as pets, and investors need to treat property as an investment. We are trying to make money – not receive awards for décor. Finally, as with all investments, sometimes we win and sometimes we lose. Just try not to bet the house.

2.0 Cycles

We all hear about cycles all the time, the real estate cycle, the business cycle, and the housing cycle. There always seems to be someone with a cycle for just about anything with a chart. Long cycles, short cycles, and in some cases imaginary cycles. What exactly is a cycle? A cycle is a pattern in data that occurred or reoccurred over time. We can only see patterns after they have happened. What causes these patterns in real estate? It really depends what we are looking for.

If we look back at the Herengracht Index, we will begin to see "patterns". The closer we look at the chart, the more we will see cyclical patterns. Approximately every four to eight years location values go up and down. Is this a cycle? Not exactly, what we are most likely witnessing is the balancing between supply and demand. Not just in real estate, but in terms of the regional economy. As we will see, it is all about balance.

2.1 Regions

A region is generally considered a metropolitan statistical area, with our major city at or near the center. The economies can be very different for each region within a country, and is driven by the demand for the regions products and services along with its ability to supply a workforce. Regions are distinguished from a country in that trade, exports, and immigration are largely unregulated – only a country can impose tariffs or protectionist measures. Citizens and companies can easily trade and move between regions. Money and profits can also move easily.

In order to understand how regions behave, researchers had broken them down to three categories, output, labor, and real estate. Output represents the export of local goods and services – shipping product out or receiving fees for services outside our region. Local consumption of goods is recycling the revenue. Funds coming from outside our region are required for economic growth. Labor is our work force. Real estate is the rental rate and supply of housing. The inter-relation of the three variables explains the value of real estate within a specific region.

Outputs, again, are local goods and services that are exported out of the region. As demand abroad for those exports grow, more jobs will be created. The region will grow. Growth from increased exports is known as demand induced growth. With demand-induced growth, incomes, and real estate rents will rise. The amount of change in each of these factors is affected by the restrictions on growth. Restrictions may be local property laws or anti-growth sentiment. Other restrictions may be geological such as a coastlines or mountain ranges.

In regions with unrestricted growth, the increases in incomes and rents will be small. However, there will be a rapid expansion of the regions size. In restricted growth regions, the income and rent increases will be much larger. The growth in the area is driven by workers with higher incomes. Instead of a rapid expansion of the region, the character of the existing real estate will change. More home amenities will be desired. In any region, the increase of incomes and housing costs will reduce the demand for the output. Employers will need to increase prices to cover the higher wages, and related increases in commercial real estate costs/rents. Not all of factors of output, income, and rents will adjust simultaneously. Income will rise faster than rent, and rent cannot rise faster than output prices. If demand for output decreases, the process will go into reverse. Incomes drop, real estate values and rents drop, and prices drop.

Regions can also grow due to a large influx of immigrants – remember Amsterdam had two such large migrations. This is known as supply induced growth and is much different from demand-induced growth. Labor has moved into the region from another, not mainly for work, but due to external events such as war or a weather related disaster. Output prices will go down as the quantity of the output rises, as long as demand remains – more jobs are created. Wages will go down as the new workers compete for employment. The degree of wage losses will exceed the price reduction in outputs. Meanwhile, demand for housing will actually cause real estate values and rents to increase.

With high demand for the regions products and services, the new immigrants will be absorbed into the workforce. The region will experience large increases in worker productivity and employment. Only a slight decline in wages and prices would occur. Real estate prices and rent would still rise due to increased residential and commercial demand.

If demand for our products and services is fixed - it is a much different outcome for the region. Most of the immigrants will not be able to be absorbed into the workforce. Output prices and wages will fall significantly. There may be a slight increase in output due to the lower prices – we create a few more low paying jobs. Real estate values and rents will rise, but modestly when compared to the demand growth scenario. In the end, many of the immigrants will leave the region to find work elsewhere.

2.1.1 Outputs: Effect on Regional Growth

A region's outputs are important. When export demands for the outputs are up, more jobs are created and new businesses move into the region or are created. Here is where the national economy plays a strong role. Interest rates, unemployment, regulations, and foreign events can affect export demand. To sum up a very complicated relationship in an over simplistic way – a rising tide raises all ships. If the tide goes down – so do the ships. No region can escape the affects of the national economy.

Over time, regions tend to specialize in certain goods and services – outputs. Due to specialization, they may experience greater growth than competing regions for a longer period. How can they achieve greater growth? Due to the composition of firms and industries in the region called the industrial mix. Regions made up of more growing industries will perform better than regions with an inferior industrial mix. It has been theorized that some of the industry growth and mix may have similar attributes to a product cycle. In a typical product cycle an item is invented, produced, and then standardized. The basic concept of the theory is as follows.

Once a new product is invented, new firms will expand rapidly to supply demand as the market begins to accept the product. Competitors and collaborators will begin to "cluster" near the firm forming a concentration of the industry. The clustering has many beneficial effects, as new products and businesses will spin off existing firms to start new companies and production. New industries will be developed, and the region will experience further rapid growth. As the prior model suggests, incomes and property values will go up. As the products become standard, producers and competitors will look for other areas where they can pay lower wages and overhead costs to increase profits. Outsourcing begins.

Let us take a quick look at an example of product cycle growth and clustering. Imagine we are back during 1950 in Palo Alto, California. The area is known as "The Valley of the Hearts' Delight". Here they grow trees to harvest prunes and apricots. After the Second World War, Stanford University had amassed a large debt due to its many expansion efforts. Looking for a solution, they conceived of an industrial park on a ranch left to them by Leland Stanford. The staff at Stanford felt they could develop the land to help solve some of the financial woes of the university. Not able to sell the land due to terms in the bequest by Leland, they would lease the land for 99-year contracts. Most importantly, only high technology companies that could benefit the university would be allowed in the development.

The Stanford Industrial Park was established, with the first facility opened in 1953. High tech companies of the day, like Hewitt Packard, soon began leasing land and building facilities. The high-tech industrial park was very successful – it was a cluster of high-tech firms. Within the next two decades, this cluster would change the world.

In 1968, a company called Intel was formed in Santa Clara nearby. In 1971 they created the first microprocessor, and the area was coined "Silicon Valley" by a local trade paper reporter. Intel then produced the first microcomputer in

2.0 Cycles

1972 – then things really get moving. The microchip industry would be launched, followed by the personal computer, microprocessors, and internet industries. Not to mention the venture capital firms. New industries and companies were born with several spin-offs. As the technologies matured, other firms in various regions and countries would compete. Eventually, some of the earlier technologies and products would move overseas to low cost manufacturers.

2.1.2 Housing

Many believe that housing prices also experience cycles. Researchers though, seem to have concluded that the housing price movements are a combination of external "shocks" and buyers/sellers expectations of housing value movement. The price movement is a markets continual attempt to come to a point of equilibrium. Supply and demand want to be equal.

To illustrate, think of a metropolitan region as a pond where a large rock is thrown in the middle. Our rock could be a positive event, such as a surge in demand for our cities products and services. Imagine the water's surface as housing prices; there we see small ripples due to wind – pricing fluctuations from the local supply and demand. Once the rock hits the water, there is a huge splash – our external shock. Initially a large wave imitates outward. Since there was only so much energy, the wave will eventually decrease in magnitude, however; the surface of the pond is now rippling up and down as the water surface tries to come to back to equilibrium. Equilibrium though can never be reached, because the world will keep chucking rocks at us.

Although dramatically oversimplified, housing prices behave similar to our pond's surface. After a positive economic shock, there is a run up (or drop if negative) in housing prices as demand suddenly increased. To meet the new demand and capitalize on the higher prices, new homes will be built to add to the housing supply. Due to a variety of reasons, developers will supply more homes than there is demand for – prices drop. At some point, the prices reach a level where buyers will begin purchasing new homes again – prices rise, and so on.

2.1.2.1 Housing Demand

In general, the demand for housing is driven by the number of households, which is a group of people living in the same dwelling. Changes in the number of households or the composition of the households indicate a change in demand. The more households that come into a region – the more dwellings required.

Demographics keep us abreast of how a regions housing market is composed. Homeowners take a basic path. First, rent a dwelling, and then eventually purchase the first home (starter home). Next, they trade-up to a larger home, and finally buy a retirement home. Along the path, the homeowner is getting older. The demographics will show the various numbers of the population that are potentially on different parts of the "path". Understanding the composition of the population and the changes within age groups can help identify changes in demand. As people age, they generally see an increase in their income. With a growing income, they are more likely to own a home, the larger the income the larger the home. Purchasing of houses of increasing value continues until people hit their mid-sixties, then retirement considerations come into play – and home values decrease. For our purposes, the demographics would show if the composition and changes in the population growth was from households and demographics with higher incomes, which could be a positive sign of home values increasing. A growth spurt from low-income households would have limited housing value increase potential.

Affordability is the throttle that governs price movement. Since most buyers finance a large portion of their home purchase, the mortgage market has a large influence on how much values can rise. Terms of the mortgage, such as interest rates and amortization schedule, will limit the amount of money buyers can borrow. If incomes are not rising, home prices cannot increase as much since fewer buyers will qualify for loans. When the economy is strong, mortgage lenders may be less risk adverse and allow higher borrowing limits anticipating rising incomes. In a down economy, the lenders would tighten their lending policies –

lower borrowing limits regardless of income. Affordability directly affects the level of housing demand.

Average sales time is a good indicator of future housing prices. The average sales time during a "normal" economy is around two to three months. A longer the sales time could indicate problems in the local or regional economy – housing prices would be expected to drop the longer a home is on the market. Shorter sales periods may indicate new demand coming into the market - we would expect prices to increase.

Although there are several other variables that could be considered, by looking at demographics, affordability, and average sales time we can get a good sense of potential market direction. To try to predict the levels of housing prices we would need to build an econometric model, which is beyond the scope this book. How does this tie back into the ripples on the pond? Our variables explain the direction of price, but do not address the volatility of the price movement. Again we will go back to the regions attempt to balance supply and demand.

Let us tie it all together. Recall that the main growth in property values comes from outside the region for our exports of goods and services – the rock thrown into the pond. The demand for exports fluctuates with the national economy. Higher demand will spur growth that will bring in new workers who will compete for local housing. Demographic data will be able to help to break down the growth into potential demand in each housing category. Regional prices adjust quickly to demand, so prices will go up the most in the housing categories with the most demand. As prices rise, builders, and developers will be enticed to develop new housing supply. At the same time, owners and realtors are seeing prices rise, and anticipate similar or slightly better pricing for their homes. Everything is going up, *at least on paper*.

As mentioned earlier, due to the nature of development the new supply tends to lag behind demand. Once prices hit an appropriate level, developers will begin building new units and subdivisions – they get overly optimistic. When demand suddenly falls, the new supply is still being put onto the market as construction is being completed. The net effect is the market becomes oversupplied with homes for sale. Average sales time on the market will begin to increase. Developers will cut prices to get rid of the left over inventory of homes – if possible. With comparable sales prices dropping, sellers will eventually need to lower their prices or stay put. Here is where it gets interesting. Prices will drop to a point where buyers will begin purchasing again. Investors begin to jump in with the buyers figuring home prices are undervalued – remember – prices tend to rise or fall to meet demand. Home prices will rise to new level, which may be much lower than the earlier highs, and may require adjustment to meet demand. As we can see, the "cycle" is really just supply continually trying to balance with demand. Pricing seems to be more of an outcome than a cause.

To forecast housing prices one must consider effects of the national economy, local economy, households, income growth, and housing supply. We need an econometric model. Running a trend line on housing prices will not work. Only models that take into account all the factors of supply and demand have a chance of correctly anticipating price movements. Although building a model seems daunting, with a bit of research most find that it is worth the effort. The math is basic, and most models can be done in a spreadsheet. The hardest part of the exercise is getting all of the data.

Luckily, today many websites and associations are continually trying to forecast housing price levels. If we cannot put our own model together, we can look to compare other econometric models. Keep in mind that we must seriously consider the source of the model and whether the results are biased. Always check more than one model, and see what assumptions are being made.

2.1.3 Speculation

Speculation is taking on higher risks to gain short-term profits. Most investments in residential real estate such as house flipping and "fixer uppers" are speculative. This is not to say that these investments are bad – they are just high risk. Understanding speculative behavior can help us to take advantage of housing price movements, especially when speculation moves into frenzy – bubbles form.

Speculation is an emotional response to positive economic shocks, and can be a prime mover of home prices. Initially home prices will rise based on the new demand created by the positive economic shock. Speculators following price trends will now have expectations that home prices will continue to rise. To reinforce their expectations many will attempt to predict future pricing trends based on past market "cycles". Once the media begins exaggerating the positive housing market, we move from a few speculators to a feeding frenzy. Everyone wants to make a quick buck. We see it on television, read about it, and hear about it at cocktail parties. The frenzy may be localized in one region. In time, it will eventually spread like a virus to contaminate other regions. Home prices will be driven up by short-term speculative forces – not rational supply and demand. So begins a bubble.

To keep the bubble growing requires the help of lending institutions. Less stringent lending practices are the equivalent to adding fuel to the fire. To keep lending and making fees, the lenders allow greater leverage for buyers to compensate for the rapidly rising home values. Excessive credit is provided. Furthermore, inflated real estate values are used as collateral for loans. This sets up a mechanism for raising home and property values. Lenders provide excess credit to buy properties with inflated prices. If prices increase further, the buyers will use the inflated price as collateral for financing to invest in another over valued property. Our initial economic shock may have started the bubble, but loose lending practices are what inflate it to its maximum limit.

Eventually, the fundamentals of supply and demand will assert themselves. Sales of homes will begin to decrease. Prices will flatten out – then fall dramatically. Buyers find they cannot sell their investment property and loose them to the banks. The lenders end up with overvalued properties that they end up selling below mortgage costs. Many lenders may go out of business. The regional and national economies will be negatively affected.

Bubbles tend to happen in assets where values are difficult to assess. This makes them common in the property markets were investors fall prey to poor pricing ability and forecasts. Nearly every country with a free property market has experienced a housing bubble at various points in history. Like it or not, bubbles will be around as long as people feel they can make a profit. For synthetic real estate, bubbles can be highly profitable, as we will cover later. What we need to focus on is where prices will move the most.

Much like normal housing values, bubbles will grow largest in areas with restricted zoning practices or physical constraints in size – think Manhattan. New supply will be difficult to bring to the market. Land to build new buildings is expensive, no thanks to our speculative behavior; and difficult governmental procedures will slow how fast the new supply can be brought to market. Therefore, existing prices will rise rapidly. At least until a glut of supply hits the market. In regions with low barriers to growth, even a bubble has a limited affect on housing prices. Supply quickly steps in to compete with existing properties so prices do not rise as much.

What are the warning signs that a bubble is occurring? Unfortunately, we will not have a definitive sign. However, we can look out for a few things. In the media, there will be a lot of positive home real estate chatter, and a lot more get rich quick gurus will have infomercials. People outside of real estate will start chatting about getting into real estate. A large number of new development announcements. If we monitor home prices, we might see home values begin to increase faster than incomes can afford. Other warning signs would be a contraction of housing sales average days on the market and months of inventory – smaller than two to three months may indicate a buying frenzy.

As the bubble begins to burst, the months of inventory will continue to grow due to new developments completing construction and coming to market. The supply will overshoot demand.

3.0 Risk vs. Reward

Speculating in residential real estate can make us a lot of money. However, as with all speculative investments, there are significant risks to be considered. The speculator's expertise, the building's features, location, and the economy will each contribute to the overall risk. Before we jump into our project examples, we must answer the most important question: "Does the project make sense?"

3.1 Feasibility

We all have heard about people flipping property at 20% and higher over the purchase price plus improvements. It sounds like they made a good investment, but what if we found out that it took two years to sell. By the time we account for closing costs, mortgage payments, and property taxes we would wonder – did they make any money?

In order to understand whether a project makes money we must examine its feasibility. A feasibility study will require us to examine required returns, property cost, renovations, carrying costs, and finally a reasonable approximation of the sales price. With reasonable inputs, the numbers will determine if the project makes sense. If we inject our emotions into the study to make the project work – the study will be useless. We have to let the numbers guide our decisions, not what we feel. So let us get to it.

"The higher the risk the greater the reward" is a common saying. It gets to the main issue of what returns a particular investment should pay. Riskier investments need to pay much higher than less risky investments. For example, U.S. Treasuries are very low risk investments that are backed by the U.S. Government. Returns on treasuries are low with an average of around 4%. At the other end of the investment risk spectrum are stocks. Most studies show that over the long haul stocks tend to produce a 10% return. Where does speculative real estate fall? Well, if our project would return only 4-5% we would be better off buying treasuries and bonds. In the 10% return level, we would prefer buying stocks. So in order to make it worth our while, we need to see a higher return for our residential real estate project. Why?

One reason we need a higher return is that real estate is typically highly leveraged. Mortgages allow buyers to purchase properties with only 10-20% of the purchase price. The higher the leverage, the less money the purchaser put into the project. Generally, this is all if not most of the money the buyer has. If they miss a paycheck or a renter does not pay, the highly leveraged buyer is at a higher risk of defaulting and loosing the property. Once the building goes into foreclosure all equity is lost. Another reason for the higher return requirement is that real estate is not liquid. An investor can buy and sell stocks and bonds with a click of a button. Residential real estate typically takes around two to three months to sell in a normal market. Sales times can take much longer if the market becomes over supplied with homes. Finally, there is uncertainty to the home's value – we will only find out how much we are paid when we sell.

So, what is a reasonable return for our speculative investment? For our answer, we will turn to the Weighted Average Cost of Capital formula known as the WACC. The WACC takes into account leverage and risk to calculate the required equity return, R_e.

$$R_e = r_p - (LTV)r_D / 1 - LTV \qquad \text{Eq. 3.1-1}$$

LTV is simply the loan to value ratio of the mortgage; r_D is the interest rate on the loan. The last variable, r_p, is the real property returns, which are generally 8%. Whoa, why did we not mention this earlier? Should we not be looking for a reasonable return between stocks and bonds? If we purchase a home all cash and rent it out over ten years – we would say yes. Speculators though are looking for short-term gains with high leverage. Therefore, we need higher returns to justify our risk. Computing required return on equity using the WACC equation:

$$R_e = (.08 - (.80).05)/(1 - .80) = 0.2 \; or \; 20\%$$

We find the equity return to make our real estate project feasible needs to be around 20%.

Jumping over to the risk side, with required return we can compare the riskiness of the different investments. Treasures are generally considered riskless around 4%. Any return required above the "riskless" return is considered the risk premium. Stocks would have a risk premium of 10% - 4% = 6%. *Speculative* residential real estate has a risk premium around 16%, nearly three times the risk of stocks.

With an estimate of our required returns, we now must determine where the market is selling to minimize our structure and location risk. We need to seek out local professionals, such as real estate brokers, to help guide us in what segments of the market are selling – three bedroom ranchers, Mc mansions, condominiums, etc. Money will be required to invest, so a realistic assessment of our ability to purchase needs to be considered. Once we have selected a market segment, we will need to back it up with numbers from comparable sales. Comparable sales are actual transactions that have taken place from similar home types. Similar not just in basic size and composition, but also similar with respect to the neighborhoods that each home resides. Remember, location value can be very different although the structural value is the same. After we have compiled at least a dozen properties, our data should give us an idea of what price our property segment is selling. Our figures will serve as a benchmark for the expected sales price and help us "back" into what we can afford to purchase.

We have our required return, and we know what housing market segment is hot and within our comfort price range. Now it is time to shop for financing. Multiple lenders should be explored to find the best deal. The maximum loan amount lenders will fork over is our actual upper bound limit of what we can afford. There may be aggressive lenders out there who can get us a larger loan, but be sure to model the loans conditions to see if it is feasible. Categorized as an investor, we will not be able to participate in most homebuyer programs. So figure we will need at least 20% of equity in the deal. After the lenders get back with us, we will have a better picture of mortgage terms and approximately how much money the banks will lend us. We are not applying for financing – we are just browsing for information.

Now we need to sit down and prepare a pro forma, which are some simple calculations that will give us a feeling for what the deal needs to be in order to be profitable. An actual quick pro forma will be shown later in the examples. Everything in our calculations needs to be approximated from a repair budget to the holding costs, such as mortgage payments. The result of our pro forma will be a guide of how much equity will be needed to purchase and fix-up the property. Furthermore, our study will also determine the total project costs and schedule. Most importantly, the pro forma will calculate the net present value of the project, the

NPV. The NPV is the present value of future cash flows minus the original investment. Using the NPV, we can determine if a project meets our investment goals. If our calculated NPV equals zero the project exactly meets our requirements, higher than zero we have excess returns. An NPV below zero means the project does not work as modeled. A great feature of using the NPV is if the value is negative, it represents the amount of costs that need to be reduced. We just need to see where we can cut costs.

Finally, it is time to hit the street and look for a deal. We need something priced at a discount that we can sell for a profit at *current* market levels. Here is where the dream begins to fade and most discover – it is not that easy. Because we know what we want to buy and how much we can afford, it will be much easier for our friendly realtor or online search engine to produce some potential properties. The broker will know more about the area and if a neighborhood is turning from good to bad. In contrast, a novice could misinterpret the same neighborhood as going from bad to good. Once the list is vetted for location issues, we will need to visit the sites. Nothing beats walking the property. We will be elated, relieved, or sorely disappointed. Although not all of us are inspectors, we should be aware of basic inspection issues that inspectors look for and take note of anything we see – better yet, a picture. Since we have visited our prospect homes, we can now narrow the list down to two or three properties. It is time for more number crunching. A pro forma should be done for each property taking into account any building maintenance issues or renovation budget revisions. We will make sure any property in consideration is able to produce a positive NPV. Each pro forma is adjusted based on our site visits. Once we are satisfied with our projections, we can begin to make offers.

Determining the feasibility of a project takes a lot of work. Most of the work needs to be done based on the market before we even begin to look for houses. Even when a house meets all of our requirements, we may lose it to competing bidders who overpay. We may not get the property simply because the owner just does not like us. In any event, armed with our feasibility work we increased our chances for a successful project.

3.2 Flipping

Flipping is buying a home at a discount and quickly selling for a profit. Sounds simple enough, but as always, nothing is as easy as it seems. First, we need to run our initial feasibility study to see what we can actually flip. We will cheat a little bit and go with the assumption that our credit is good and our income reasonable. The financing of second homes and investment properties can be trickier than a primary residence. Lenders know that they have more at risk and want to make sure we have the knowledge and ability to pull our deal off.

For this example, let us suppose we found that the majority of sales are for three bedrooms with two baths. These ranch style homes are selling in the $150,000 to $200,000 price range. Unfortunately, we only have $20,000 to use as a down payment, which would limit us to under $100,000 once we factor in closing and carrying costs. Unless we can find a lender at a higher loan to value ratio or a partner, we will need to look for cheaper houses.

After visiting several banks and crying on the phone to our realtor, we find that there is some life in the lower home price brackets. The sales times on the market are within a reasonable two to three months. However, the banks are considering us investors and will require 20% cash equity. Let us run a preliminary feasibility to see where we need to be.

Per our preliminary pro forma (See Figure 3.2-A), we find that we can afford to purchase properties in the $67,000 range. The lender will lend on the purchase price, we must pay for the closing costs, maintenance, and renovations. Therefore, those costs need to be deducted from our equity. This affects the actual down payment toward the property. Our timeframe is limited to six months from purchase to sale. Six months is reasonable taking into account the average time of sale at 2 to 3 months plus an additional 3 months to purchase and renovate the property. Plugging in the sales costs and the required return, we find that our property needs to sell just over $108,900.

Quick Pro Forma - Flipping a House

Our Total Equity		$	20,000.00
Total Project Schedule (months)			6

Mortgage Info:
Loan Amount		$	53,345.73
LTV			80.0%
Interest Rate			4.0%
Loan Term (yrs)			20
Mortgage Constant			0.07358

Property Costs:
Purchase Price Target		$	66,682.17
Renovation Budget	5%	$	3,334.11

Other Costs:
Purchasing Cost	5%	$	3,334.11
Utilities & Maintenance		$	700.00
Property Taxes - pro rated		$	666.82
Mortgage payments		$	1,962.64
Selling Cost	4%	$	2,667.29
Total Costs		$	76,679.84

Required Equity Return:	20%	$	4,000.00
Sales Price Target:		$	108,890.13
Gain in Total Value:			39%
NPV for Equity			$0.05

Figure 3.2-A, The house example pro forma for a flip.

Armed with our pro forma, we will work with our realtor to find homes selling around $67,000 with the appropriate building features in neighborhoods where home prices are around $109,000. After studying a list of potential properties, we visit our best candidates making sure that our renovation budget is reasonable. If everything checks out and the seller is reasonable we would commence to purchase, renovate, and *hope* to sell the home at a profit.

Looking back at the pro forma, we notice we purchased a home at $66,700 and flipped it six months later for $108,890. The difference in price would calculate to a gain in property value of 39%, however; we only made our required return of 20%. Out of the additional value, only $4,000 is actual profit. The remaining monies are eaten up by costs. What is our net present value? It is zero. To determine the NPV we need to estimate the project costs in each month. Because the calculation is sensitive to time, it is important to allocate the costs in the correct period. When accounting for the project time between cash outlays and final payment, we see that the project just makes our investment goal.

As we can see, we have expended a lot of effort over six months for our $4,000 profit. This equates to roughly $670 for each month, or equal to taking a part time job that pays $8 an hour. In order to make more money we would need to increase the value of the properties we flip or flip more homes – in any event, we need more money. We have taken on a lot of financial risk and worked hard for a seemingly small reward. However, it should be noted that a 20% return on our $20,000 investment in six months would be unlikely in stocks and bonds.

If we are successful in our first flip, we will repeat the process and flip homes with increasingly higher value. The higher the home value the larger the return, and money is the reason we got into the game in the first place. As long as the market for homes increases in value, we may be fortunate enough to ride the market upswing. Most speculators will graduate from fixer-uppers to Mc Mansions. All seems rosy until the market suddenly turns down. If we find ourselves in the middle of a renovation, we could be in for a rough time. Sales time could dramatically increase and home prices could drop. Without a hedge, we are fully exposed to the market.

3.3 Rental Homes

Income property is different from flipping. Instead of hoping to profit quickly from property value gains, we are depending upon long-term rental income and growth. Rental property is an investment. The income of the property should provide enough income to cover expenses and perhaps some profit. We do not realize the full investment return until we sell the property, which could be in one to ten years. There are numerous tax benefits associated with rental property that allow much of the finance interest and depreciation to be deducted. However, we will have to pay back most of the deductions when we sell. The depreciation is recaptured.

Many of the same feasibility considerations will be done for rental property, but there is one major difference. The value of the property is based upon its current income and the markets future expectation for income growth. A quick way to estimate the true value of a rental property is by dividing the net operating income by its capitalization rate. To determine the net operating income, NOI, we simply subtract all of the expenses from the gross income. The capitalization rate, CAP, is a figure that relates to the property's yield and riskiness. With a CAP rate of 8%, we would expect to make a yearly yield of 8% from the income. A riskier property asset should have a higher CAP rate than a less risky asset. Determining the correct CAP rate will require research. If we are looking at renting a single home, we are going to have to compute the CAP by taking estimated rental incomes and dividing by the comparable recorded sales prices of similar properties. Nationally the median CAP for the rental housing is around 9% over time. Additionally, research needs to be done to determine what the rental and vacancy rates are for our property segment.

3.0 Risk vs. Reward

Five Year Pro Forma Income Statement

COST & REVENUE ASSUMPTIONS		FINANCE ASSUMPTIONS			KEY RATIOS	
Land	9,000	Total Cost	100.0%	90,236	Total Square Feet	1,200.00
Building	76,236	Owner Eq.	22.2%	20,000	Ave. Sq Ft/Unit	1,200.00
Improvements	3,000	Rq'd Loan	77.8%	70,236	Ave. Rent/Sq Ft	0.89
Closing Costs	2,000				Ave. Cost/Sq Ft	75.20
Total	90,236				Ave. Unit Cost	90,235.77
			Annual	Monthly	CAP Rate	10.1%
Number of Units	1	Int. Rate	5.00%	0.417%	GRM	7.47
Average Monthly Rent	1,064	Term	20	240	Expense/Unit	2,973.19
Gross Monthly Revenues	1,064	Payment	5,636	470	Expenses/Foot	2.48
Estimated Growth Rate Projections			3.00%	3.00%	3.00%	2.50%	2.50%
Average Monthly Rent				1096	1129	1163	1192	1222

				PROJECTED			
OPERATING REVENUES		Monthly	Year 1	Year 2	Year 3	Year 4	Year 5
Gross Potential Income	88.0%	1,064	13,156	13,550	13,957	14,306	14,663
Losses to Vacancy	5.0%	55	658	678	698	715	733
Collection Losses	1.8%	20	237	244	251	258	264
Losses to Concessions	3.3%	36	434	447	461	472	484
Rent Revenue Collected	98.1%	954	11,827	12,182	12,547	12,861	13,182
Other Income	1.9%	20	250	257	265	272	279
Gross Income	100.0%	974	12,077	12,439	12,812	13,133	13,461
OPERATING EXPENSES							
Insurance	5.0%	53	658	678	698	715	733
Taxes	2.0%	21	263	271	279	286	293
Marketing	1.9%	20	250	257	265	272	279
Contract Services	9.0%	96	1,184	1,220	1,256	1,288	1,320
Repair & Maintenance	4.7%	50	618	637	656	672	689
Total Op. Expenses	22.6%	241	2,973	3,062	3,154	3,233	3,314
NOI	77.4%	733	9,104	9,377	9,658	9,900	10,147
Interest on Loan		293	3,512	3,406	3,294	3,177	3,054
Dep. Exp. - Building		231	2,772	2,772	2,772	2,772	2,772
Dep. Exp. - Equipment		-	-	-	-	-	-
Net Income Before Taxes		210	2,820	3,199	3,592	3,950	4,321
Income Tax Rate	35.0%	73	987	1,120	1,257	1,383	1,512
Net Income After Taxes		136	1,833	2,079	2,335	2,568	2,809
CASH FLOW FROM OPERATIONS							
Net Income After Taxes		136	1,833	2,079	2,335	2,568	2,809
Depreciation Expense		231	2,772	2,772	2,772	2,772	2,772
Total Cash Flow from Operations		367	4,605	4,852	5,107	5,340	5,581
Interest on Loan		293	3,512	3,406	3,294	3,177	3,054
Total Cash Available for Loan Servicing		660	8,117	8,257	8,401	8,517	8,635
Debt Service		470	5,636	5,636	5,636	5,636	5,636
Remaining After Tax CF from Ops.		190	2,481	2,621	2,765	2,881	2,999
CF/ DSCR			1.41	1.44	1.47	1.49	1.51	1.53

Figure 3.3-A, Rental property pro forma *(continues on next page)*.

Synthetic Real Estate Investment

SALES COMPUTATIONS							
Terminal Cap Rate:	9%	Sales Cost: 3%		Tax Rate: 15%		Recovery: 25%	
		Exit Price	Sale Cost	Acc. Dep.	Loan Repay	Before Tax	After Tax
Estimated Exit Price/Gain on Sale - 1 Yr		101,153	3,035	2,772	68,112	27,234	24,448
Estimated Exit Price/Gain on Sale - 3 Yr		107,313	3,219	8,317	63,540	32,237	27,114
Estimated Exit Price/Gain on Sale - 5Yr		112,746	3,382	13,861	58,499	37,004	29,654

AFTER TAX INVESTMENT PERFORMANCE							
Net CF's from Investment - 1 Yr Exit		(20,000)	26,929				
Net CF's from Investment - 3 Yr Exit		(20,000)	2,481	2,621	29,879		
Net CF's from Investment - 5 Yr Exit		(20,000)	2,481	2,621	2,765	2,881	32,653
Estimated WACC:	20.0%						
Annualized IRR - 1 Yr	34.65%	NPV - 1 Yr		2,034		ROI - 1 Yr	12.4%
Annualized IRR - 3 Yr	22.56%	NPV - 3 Yr		982		ROI - 3 Yr	13.8%
Annualized IRR - 5 Yr	20.00%	NPV - 5 Yr		(0)		ROI - 5 Yr	15.0%

Figure 3.3-B, Rental property pro forma continued.

Now we have gathered our information on local rental rates, vacancies, and estimated the capitalization rate. We need to determine what the return on our equity needs to be to justify the project. For financing income property, some lenders will go as high as a 90% loan to value. However, since the mortgage will not cover the renovation and closing costs, we should still figure an equity requirement of 20%. Our required return is still around 20%, but the return needs to be considered across the projects timeline from purchase to sale. Again, we will utilize the NPV calculation.

As seen in the pro forma, rental property is a bit more complicated than flipping a house. Each year we need forecast revenues and expenses. Growth rates for both will also need to be estimated for each year. Next, tax benefits must be considered to calculate our true income after taxes. Finally, we compute our investment performance and see if our model meets our hurdles utilizing the NPV.

With our feasibility study, we would look to purchase a rental home priced around $85,000 (add the land and building costs) with the structural features required such as number of rooms and baths. Rental rates where prospect properties are located need to be near $1,000 per month. The improvement budget is set at $3,000. Our properties being considered will need to be in reasonably good shape. No major renovations allowed. Armed with our numbers, we can go in search of potential candidates.

Rental property requires management to meet our financial objectives. Once we purchase the property, we need to get it occupied and cash flowing. Tenants will need to be screened, and the facilities need to be maintained. Poor management will increase vacancy and the overall income and value of the property. We need to stay on top of things. Professional property managers can be hired to take care of tenants and maintenance, but it costs money and our overall investment performance will suffer. If we do not wish to manage our properties, we need to account for the additional expense. Renting property is a people business as much as bricks and mortar.

Let us pretend it is five years later and our pro forma is now a financial statement. The net operating income, NOI, each year averages around $9,000. After debt and taxes, we are left with about $2,500 per year of income. Actual income is around 2% of the total project costs or 10% of the invested equity at risk. The actual investment performance of the property is not realized until it is sold. The returns are very sensitive to these price movements. To illustrate, we figured to make our investment goal of 20% the property would sell at a 9% CAP rate. In year five, this would equate to $112,750. If we had underestimated the CAP rate and the property sold for a 10% CAP, $101,470; we would see our 20% return reduced to 13.9%. A one percent change in the CAP – an almost entirely emotional value based on future expectations – can move our returns as much as 30%.

3.4 Overview

Hundreds of books are written on how to flip homes or invest in rental property. We have glazed the surface of each subject to understand the basic mechanics of physical real estate investment. It takes a lot of research and legwork to produce a successful project, but nothing worthwhile is easy. Unfortunately, with all of our work we could still be wrong. Humans are bad at forecasting future events, and our emotions tend to get the best of us. Each piece of information we gathered and placed in our feasibility studies are subject to error and bias. Even with correct variable estimates today, our future projections can be wildly off. Why? The future cannot be predicted, and we will be either beneficiaries or martyrs to future events. All we can really hope to accomplish is to limit risk as much as possible, specifically management and market risk.

Management risk is hard to quantify directly, but our decisions have dramatic impacts on our projects. Flipping homes and buying rental properties require that we are able to determine the correct market segment and price levels. In actuality, nobody knows what real estate is worth since the values are constantly moving. Until we gain enough experience we can mistakenly overpay for properties. Deals may end up as disasters.

Another common management error is misinterpreting renovation costs and requirements. Less experienced speculators and investors are caught up in the design instead of watching the budget. Renovations produce additional value to the home as a lesser percentage of their costs with 90% being on the higher end of returns. We need only spend what is needed to sell or rent the property.

Finally, we may have euphemistic future expectations of value and rental income growth. Nobody invests to lose money, so it is reasonable to assume that investors looking to flip or rent properties are a bit optimistic. Being eager to deal, some folks will take shortcuts and look at price and rental trends to make their projections. We tend to look at past performance and anticipate similar future results. However, as mentioned earlier – property value moves based on economics, not past prices. Rental growth also moves with the economy, but it rarely goes up much over time when it is adjusted for inflation; in fact, it is virtually flat. Our future expectations if too lofty can cause us to overpay for sites, and take on risky projects that currently look reasonable.

The market is the tide that raises all boats or sinks them. The longer the project timeline, the greater exposure we have to a negative market movement. House flipping in particular is very sensitive to the market. If there is not enough demand to sell the home quickly, the projects lose money. Rental homes are also at risk. If homes begin to flood the market, many owners turn to renting them at any cost. Additionally, when home demand is down apartment demand is similarly down – the economy is probably on the decline and workers are leaving. We may find that our income does not cover costs, and need to find supplemental funds to carry the property.

This is a risky business. Management risk can be managed through experience. Market risk, as we will learn later, can be minimized through hedging.

Part 2

The Derivatives

"Lions, and tigers, and bears! Oh my!"

– Dorothy, The Wizard of Oz

4.0 A Brief History of Derivatives

In finance, a derivative is an agreement based on an underlying asset. Instead of exchanging the actual asset, agreements are made to exchange cash or other assets for the underlying asset within a specified timeframe. As the value of the underlying asset changes, so does the value of the derivative. Following the definition, we find that our lives are filled with derivatives. Credit cards, service agreements, and many other everyday contracts promise a service now in exchange for cash within the billing period – the specified period. Rather than being the boogey man of financial destruction, derivatives are financial tools that if used properly make our lives easier. History shows that these financial instruments were developed to solve real world issues that needed to be solved for business.

4.1 Ancient History

Although generally thought of as a high tech trading tool, derivatives have been around for a quite a while. Over 100,000 years ago, it is known that people bartered for goods and services. The problem with bartering is that it is hard to trade between items that are harvested at different times of year. Items that perished quickly are difficult to trade. The solution was to begin utilizing a less or non-perishable commodity such as wine, grains, or other objects as an intermediary. For instance, we could trade a perishable item for wine, which we could then use to exchange for another crop harvested later in the year – our currency being effectively wine. These types of trades eventually led to the development of commodity money, an intermediate store of value that expanded the number of trading opportunities. Almost every civilization would develop a commodity money basis for trading.

Around 8,000 B.C. writing and mathematics had developed in Sumer, located in the Tigris and Euphrates river region, to a point they developed a unique method for accounting. Clay tokens were used to represent the different commodities and quantities (See Picture 4.1-1). To keep people from tampering with the tokens, they baked them into a hollow vessel. Pressed into the exterior of the vessel – prior to baking – would be markings similar to the tokens inside and a witness mark to make it official. The beauty of this system is the way it resolves disputes. If there were any disagreement of the values on the exterior of the vessel,

4.0 A Brief History of Derivatives

Picture 4.1-1, Globular envelope with a cluster of accounting tokens. Source, photo by Marie-Lan Nguyen

they would break it open to count the tokens inside. Eventually the tokens and vessels would become a promise to deliver a quantity of goods by a certain date – all baked on the vessel. Now instead of wine, we would accept a vessel and give the other party (counterparty) our product. Then based on the quantity and time of delivery pressed into the vessel, we would receive the counterparty's goods. By 3,500 B.C., new forms of writing and math enabled the

Sumerians to replace the vessels with clay tablets. These trades are similar in behavior to forward contracts.

A forward contract is an agreement where a seller agrees to deliver an item by a certain date to a buyer at an agreed price. Typically, forward contracts are settled upon the delivery of the item at the expiration date. Profits are only realized if the buyer had purchased the item at a reasonable price. If the buyer overpaid they would lose money.

In ancient Greece, the Athenians used shipping contracts for trading which resemble forward contracts, with a twist. The buyer would borrow the money up front. Prior to a trading voyage, an entrepreneur (buyer) looking to profit on a trade of commodities would make an agreement with a merchant who would finance the voyage. They would draw up a contract. The contract would state the amount of money loaned and required interest the entrepreneur would pay the merchant upon return. Since these voyages were risky, the merchants demanded a high return in the rage of 30%. After all, there were many ways a ship could disappear; pirates, unfriendly nations, and storms to name but a few. Further stipulations would name the commodity to be purchased, state where it was to be purchased, the ships route, and a time limit for the voyage. To make sure the entrepreneurs' would not cheat them, the merchants had a trustworthy acquaintance or employee accompany the voyage. Upon reaching the agreed upon port of call, our entrepreneurs' would purchase the commodity – or sell in the case of exports. In either event, the merchant now had an effective ownership of the commodities until they were paid back. The similarity to a forward contract can be seen since the factors of price, commodity, and time are stipulated in the shipping contract. Profits for the entrepreneurs' would only be realized if they could sell the commodity at a high enough price to cover the merchant's loan and interest. If they could not cover the loan, they would end up in court and may find much of their collateral, and perhaps their freedom, in jeopardy. Because trade was so important, laws and regulations would develop to ensure each party would be justly treated in disputes.

4.2 Medieval Europe

Around 1100 European merchants developed the "fair letter" that acted like a letter of credit between the buyer and seller. These letters would then be settled at regional trade fairs such as the Fairs of Champagne; an annual cycle of trading fairs held in town located in the Champagne and Brie regions of France, which were the main markets for Northern Europe. The seller would have the merchandise ready for pickup at a fair, and the buyer would give a "fair letter" for payment. The Fairs of Champagne started out as mainly agricultural events, but evolved into major trading markets for many commodities. Italian moneychangers at the fair would settle the letters for the merchants. The Fairs of Champagne became international clearinghouses for paper debt and credit. The seller would receive another "fair letter" or letter of credit that could be settled in or near their hometown with a local goldsmith. Back in these times, the local goldsmith is where merchants held their money. The goldsmiths would eventually evolve into banks. Over time, the fairs began to lose their dominance in trade. Many of the trade routes to the fairs were over land. War and political issues would cause over land routes to fall from favor – traders turned to sea routes. The fairs would move from the Champagne region to the port city of Burges.

Bruges is interesting because of the impact natural changes in the environment had on the city and its economy. Bruges is located near the North Sea in modern day Belgium. Prior

4.0 A Brief History of Derivatives

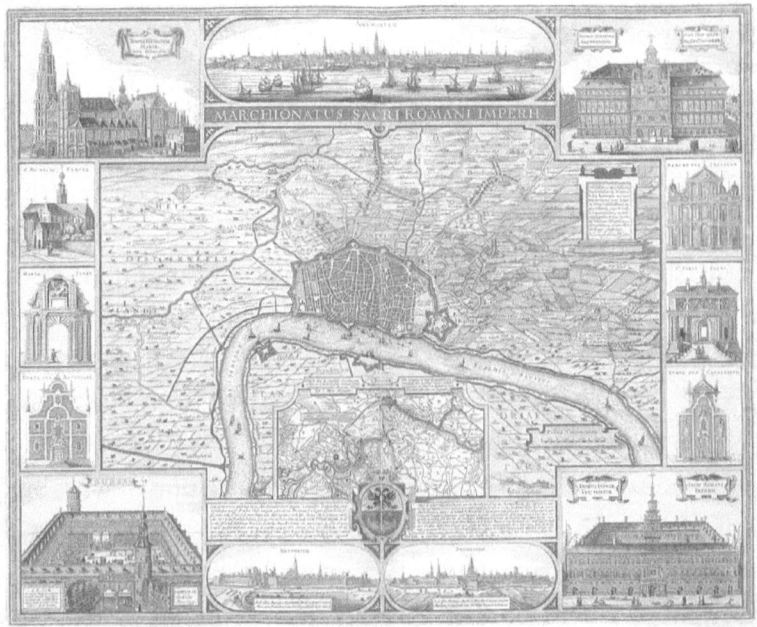

Figure 4.2-A, Antwerp map circa 1624.

to 1134, the natural water channels that provided access to the sea had silted up. That year a large storm hit the coast and reopened the natural channels near the city. Soon, because of the over land trade issues for the Fairs of Champagne, merchants started using the port city as their main trading location. Ships would begin to arrive from as far away as the Mediterranean. By 1309 Bruges became one of the most sophisticated money markets and trading cities in Europe. Growth and prosperity seemed abundant until around 1500. The channels that had been the reason for Bruges success began to silt in. Trade would move to another port city – Antwerp. Bruges would decline.

In 1515, the city of Antwerp opens the Bourse, a dedicated building where local and international traders could gather to conduct business. Before the Bourse, traders generally met at a specified place and time to conduct their affairs. Now there was a dedicated marketplace year round. Soon, the town of Antwerp grew dramatically as the Bourse became the preferred place of trade in Northern Europe. Textiles from England, spices from the Portuguese, and metals from Germany all were traded in Antwerp. Due to its success, by 1531 a new and larger Bourse was built outside the city in a planned development specifically with trade in mind. Away from the port and warehouses, the new facility is where contracts and other financial instruments were traded. Traders were not purchasing commodities directly; they were buying and selling rights to commodities - intangibles. A true financial market had been established.

Antwerp was generally prosperous until 1648. Antwerp is located on the Scheldt River. The river provided access to the ocean and allowed the city to become an international trading post. Recall that the region was in the middle of the Eighty Years War, which ended in 1648. Antwerp was located in the southern provinces of the Netherlands that remained under control of Spain – the Spanish Netherlands. As part of the Treaty of Munster, the peace treaty between Spain and the United Provinces (Dutch Republic), the

Scheldt River would be closed to navigation. Antwerp's trading activities were effectively shut down. Amsterdam would become the new leading trading hub for Northern Europe.

For the next two hundred years the trading of commodities in the western world will utilized agreements that are similar to forward contracts. Several civilizations would have similar type of agreements or arrangements for trading not only for ship voyages, but for caravans as well. However, the agreements are still generally between parties that must deal with each other directly, sort of an ancient over-the-counter (OTC). Each party must trust the other party in order to trade. The next revolution in trading would occur in the East.

4.3 A Major Step Forward

In Feudal Japan around 1700, many rulers in agricultural regions taxed their subjects in rice. For currency, they would bring the rice to cities such as Osaka where it was stored and sold at auction. Only authorized wholesalers were allowed to bid on the rice at auction. The winning bidder would receive a rice voucher that would be settled shortly thereafter for cash. The vouchers eventually became transferable; a new market in the buying and selling of vouchers would develop among the merchants.

Around 1730, the Dojima Rice Exchange is established with the full support of the government. At the exchange, there are two types of rice markets; the shomai and choaimai. The shomai market is where actual rice trading takes place. Here traders buy and sell different grades of rice based on the spot price. Rice vouchers are issued for each transaction and would be settled within four days. At the choaimai the first future market was operating. Choaimai roughly translates to rice trading on books. In the spring, summer, and fall different grades of rice were contracted with standardized agreements. No cash or vouchers were exchanged; all relevant information was recorded in a book at a clearinghouse. The contract period was limited to four months at a time. All contracts had to be settled prior to the closing of the contract period, and no contract was allowed to carry over to another period. Settlement of the differences in value between the current rice spot price and the contract had to be done with cash or an opposing contract position. With a few interruptions and updates, the rice exchanges would operate until 1937.

To be able to participate in the exchange, traders were required to establish lines of credit with a clearinghouse. Trades were done through the clearinghouse, and if the trader defaulted on a trade, the clearinghouse was responsible for payment. Similar to today, the clearinghouse acts as the intermediary and guarantees payment on trades. Hence, the Dojima Rice Exchange is considered by many to be the first futures market. The final metamorphosis in commodities trading and derivatives would be over a century after the establishment of the rice exchange in the New World.

4.4 The New World

Receiving its city charter in 1837, Chicago had grown to over 4,000 inhabitants. Soon four events would lay the groundwork for this small city to become one of the world's largest. The year is 1848 and the Illinois and Michigan Canal has just been finished to connect the Great Lakes to the Mississippi River and ultimately the Gulf of Mexico. That same year the telegraph is introduced – within two years Chicago would be connected to most major East Coast cities. Also in 1848, railroad companies install lines for commerce; the city will become a large railroad hub. Lastly, the Chicago Board of Trade (CBOT) was founded.

Prior to the exchange, commodity trading operated similar to earlier centuries. Buyers and sellers would need to locate each other then make an agreement – similar to a forward contract. The problem was if the prices fluctuated too much the other party would back out of the deal, there was significant counter-party risk. As earlier fairs and markets, the CBOT was founded to make it easier to trade and bring order to the process. Initially the CBOT was a voluntary association with little active trading activity. By 1850, the exchange had developed rules and product standards, which allowed the grain market to operate more efficiently, but forward contracts were still in use. Since contracts were assignable, speculators began to play the commodities markets looking to cash in on price movements. In 1855, France moved its grain purchasing from New York to Chicago; CBOT had become a very popular place to trade in grains. The Illinois State Legislature incorporated the exchange in 1859. The true revolution in commodity trading for the CBOT would not take place until 1865. That year standardized agreements were introduced with the exchange as the counter party – futures agreements. This is similar in nature to what the Japanese were doing 130 years earlier.

1898, The Chicago Board of Trade spun off the Chicago Butter and Egg Board, which would evolve into the Chicago Mercantile Exchange by 1919. Over time, each exchange would begin trading a broad range of product types from agricultural commodities to metals. Major advances in trading derivatives would not come until 1970's. Perhaps not so coincidentally, this period also gives birth to the microprocessor and personal computers. It is the beginning of the Computer Age.

4.5 The Computer Age

The 1970's is when derivatives gained widespread use. Several factors were at play to propel derivative markets. First, many governments began to deregulate pricing and controls in markets introducing higher volatility. Tedious calculations were required utilizing probability theories to help predict future price movements. Luckily, at this time the computer becomes more wide spread allowing the complex models and computations to be solved quickly and efficiently. Then in 1973, Fischer Black and Myron Scholes would publish their paper, "The Pricing of Options and Corporate Liabilities", which established methodologies to help determine option prices. The paper also shows using options on equities that it is possible to create a hedged position – something fairly well known in agricultural commodities. That same year and coincidentally, the Chicago Board of Trade opens the Chicago Board Options Exchange. With a methodology to price options, computers to crunch the numbers, and a market to trade– things boomed. Over the next few decades, there would be derivatives on almost anything with a market willing to trade.

The next big development for derivatives would be electronic trading. Launched initially by the Chicago Mercantile Exchange in 1992, electronic trading has gained wide acceptance. Benefits have been greater liquidity, reduced transaction cost, and higher transparency. Today, trading in virtually any derivative, commodity, or security can be done from one's living room.

4.6 Property Derivatives

The tools we utilize for synthetic real estate are property derivatives. Similar to forward agreements in concept, property derivatives have been around for millennia. In fact, a simple contract to buy a home is a forward agreement – buyer and seller agree upon the price and period for delivery (due diligence period). The due diligence period could be equated to determining if the property's "grade/quality" meets your contract requirements. As we sometimes learn most painfully, the price we pay may not be what the true value of the real estate is. Real estate, unlike many other commodities, comes in many prices, sizes, and locations. Before efficient markets develop, there would need to be a reasonable "standardization" of property values – an index. Looking to fill the information gap, several institutions, businesses, and academia worked on developing indices for their interests. The results of these efforts would yield indices for commercial and residential real estate with the first indices appearing around 1980.

With the development of reliable property value indexes, the first early attempt of a property derivative market began in London around 1994. Focusing on commercial real estate, the market for property derivatives never really caught on with investors. In 2005, property derivatives came back to life in the U.K. with trades on commercial property. Although many various derivative types were available, the most common type of transaction would be in swaps and eventually forward agreements.

The United States would not really get started in property derivatives until around 2005. Very similar to practices in London, the market is for the most part an over the counter affair although a market for pricing does exist. Different derivative types, but mostly forwards on the index, are available for residential and commercial indices. A bright spot for residential investment came in 2006 with CME/Chicago Board of Trade establishing a market for housing futures based on the S&P/ Case-Shiller Index – although trading is light, it is really the only market where real estate futures can be electronically traded.

Most recently, June 2009, equities (stocks) had been developed to allow traders to effortlessly invest or hedge real estate risk – allowing even greater access to property derivatives for small investors since equity-trading accounts have smaller deposit requirements. Known as MacroShares, they had great potential. Unfortunately, they suspended trading in January 2010. Trading did not take off as expected. Perhaps they were an unfortunate victim of timing; trying to launch a real estate investment product in the middle of a depression.

5.0 Real Estate Indices

In synthetic real estate, we trade property derivatives that are valued based on an index. The index value represents real property values based on market forces for a country or specific region. It is not possible to gage individual property value from an index, but it is possible to get a sense of regional property values in relation to subsequent periods – a benchmark. In effect, synthetic real estate does not rely on a single property but all properties represented by a real estate index.

Today there are real estate indices that cover a broad range of commercial and residential real estate in various geographical regions and countries. In the United States, there are three main indices. The National Council of Real Estate Investment Fiduciaries Property Index (NPI) for commercial real estate, and for residential real estate there is Radar Logic's RPX and the S&P/Case-Shiller.

5.1 NPI – Commercial Real Estate Index

The need for an index was felt by commercial real estate investors back in the 1970's. Stocks and other financial investments had broad time series of data which to study. Real estate did not have a reliable index of property value, probably because of the difficulty inherent in property investment. Buildings are mostly heterogeneous, and "trade" infrequently. Making an index would require that all properties would need to be standardized – no easy task. Undaunted, the real estate investors set about to create an index. Their results would culminate in the launching of the Frank Russell Company Property Index (FRC Property Index) in 1981. In 1982, the NCREIF was established to allow greater industry involvement in the index; they would now jointly collect and publish the index with the Frank Russell Company. Membership in NCREIF grew to include all aspects of the commercial real estate industry – from investors to academia. With growth in membership came more buildings to collect data. Soon, the index's name was changed to the Russell-NCREIF Property Index. Finally, by 1994 the NCREIF was a fully functional association able to collect and compile the index independently. They assumed responsibility for the index and would rename it the NCREIF Property Index; know now as the NPI. Today, the NPI is the main U.S. commercial real estate index.

Data used for compiling the NPI are provided by Data Contributing Members of the NCREIF. The data for qualifying properties are submitted quarterly in compliance

5.0 Real Estate Indices

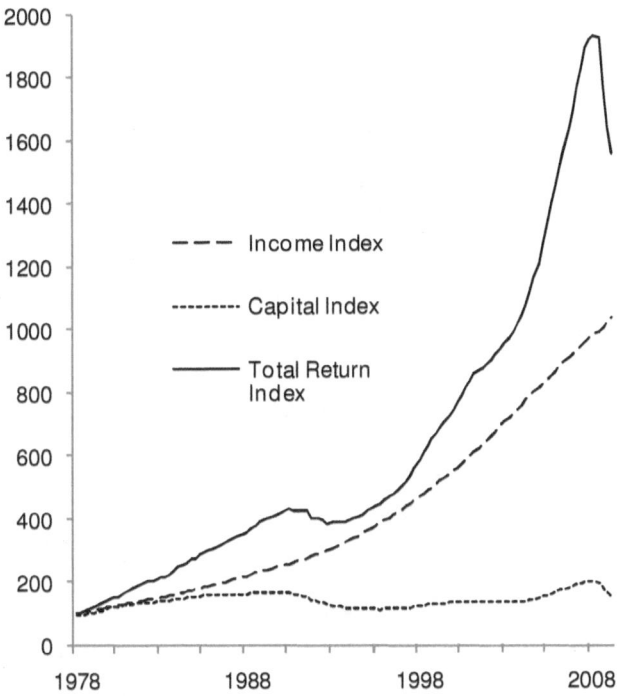

Figure 5.1-A, NCREIF NPI Indices.

with the requirements of the real estate information standards. An independent appraisal is required for each property every three years. To be considered as a qualifying property, the property must be operational with at least 60% occupancy. All properties must be owned or controlled by a qualified tax-exempt institutional investor or agent. Only apartments, hotels, industrial, office, and retail buildings are eligible. At the beginning of the index in 1977, only 233 properties were included with a total value of $580 million. At the end of 2009, the index measures the results of 6,186 properties with a total value of $243.8 trillion.

The NPI represents the quarterly total returns of a large representative pool of income producing investment grade properties. Three components make up the index – income return, capital value, and total value. The Income Return is the quarterly net income divided by the estimated expenses, represented in the formula:

$$IR = \frac{(NOI)}{\left(BV + \frac{1}{2}CI - \frac{1}{2}PS - \frac{1}{3}NOI\right)}$$

Eq. 5.1-1

BMV is the beginning market value, CI is capital improvements, and PS is partial sales. Notice it is not an actual income value, but a ratio that takes into account quarterly costs such as partial sales of property (i.e., selling an out parcel of land) and capital improvements in the denominator. Capital value is similarly handled as a ratio to measure changes in property value. In the equation below, EMV represents the end market value. The denominator takes consideration of improvements and partial sales, per the following:

$$CV = \frac{(EMV - BMV) + PS - CI}{\left(BMV + \frac{1}{2}CI - \frac{1}{2}PS - \frac{1}{3}NOI\right)}$$

Eq. 5.1-2

5.0 Real Estate Indices

For the total value we add the income return and capital value.

The equations have been set up to simulate that the property was bought and sold during the quarter being evaluated; they are calculating the internal rate of return (IRR) for the quarter. Capital improvements and partial sales are all estimated to take place mid-quarter. Subtracting 1/3 of the NOI is done in the denominator because the income is received monthly. The reduction adjusts the solution to account for the monthly income payments.

All contributing properties have their income returns, capital value, and total value computed. A weight factor is then calculated based on the market value of the property against other properties in the index. The higher the market value, the greater the properties influence on the index. The weights are used to compile and compute a value for the entire data set. The new values are then added to the prior quarter index value. Initially in the fourth quarter of 1977, the index was set at 100. Since then the above calculations have been made and the index adjusted (See Figure 5.1-A).

A particularly interesting pattern exists in the index data. If we plot the income and capital value ratios each quarter, the result is not as smooth as the index would lead us to believe, (See Figure 5.1-B). Remember that the index value was set at 100, and then the returns are added to that number. With only the returns, we get a better feel for how

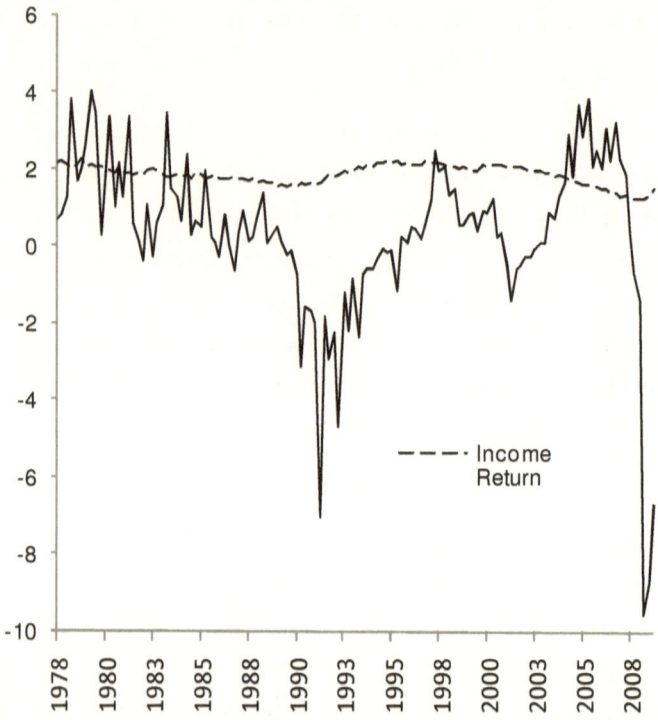

Figure 5.1-B, Income Returns and Capital Values.

the constitute components are behaving. Our next chart shows the quarterly changes in the income return and capital values. The plot is not cumulative; it shows the change in the values for each period. On the chart, we see that the income ratio is not very volatile. Each quarter the income return seems to hover around two percent. The capital value, on the other hand, is highly volatile. Capital values reflect the appraisers and markets *opinion* of property value. As we can see, they seem to change their minds frequently. What can we derive from this?

When future growth in income is *expected*, the market values the income properties higher and vice versa. The higher appraised values are shown on the chart when the capital value line is positive. In addition, although the index is weighted for a broad sample of properties, it also shows that incomes grow at an average rate of two percent a year. Interestingly enough, inflation also averages a growth rate of around two percent. Therefore, we see that of the investment grade properties that comprise the index, growth tends to match inflation. It would seem that future expectations might play a large part in capital values since income growth does not seem to change much.

Property derivatives, such as swaps and forwards, are available on the NPI for the total return index. Trading is done over the counter with financial institutions utilizing standardized agreements between the parties. Total contract amounts, also known as the notional amount, are large with trades generally above $5 million. Due to counter party risk, the financial institutions are very cautious to make sure the counter party can live up to the contractual obligations – good and bad. With high priced contracts and credit requirements, NCREIF total return property index trades are made primarily by larger companies and institutions.

Other types of derivatives, such as future contracts are being planned. Future contracts would allow smaller investors to take up synthetic positions for commercial property, greatly expanding their investment opportunities.

5.2 Radar Logic's RPX

With efforts going back to 2003, Radar Logic launched the Radar Logic Price Index (RPX) in 2007 for property derivative trading. The index is a composite index that covers residential real estate sales based on current transactions in twenty-five major metropolitan statistical areas (MSA's). All residential properties and legitimate sales are considered to include condominiums, new homes, and foreclosures.

RPX MSA's Tracked				
Atlanta	Boston	Charlotte	Chicago	Cleveland
Columbus	Denver	Detroit	Jacksonville	Las Vegas
Los Angeles	Miami	Milwaukee	Minneapolis	New York
Philadelphia	Phoenix	Sacramento	San Diego	San Francisco
San Jose	Seattle	St. Louis	Tampa	Washington, D.C.

Table 5.2-A

The RPX indices reflect current home values on a dollar per square foot basis. Each day transaction data is taken from the appropriate municipality. A small bit of a time lag is in the data since we are seeing data when it is published by the government, not on the actual transaction day. Next, a distribution is calculated from the data to establish the day's index level. The distribution takes the last consecutive three hundred and sixty-five days of data plus the current day. From the day's transaction data and the

5.0 Real Estate Indices

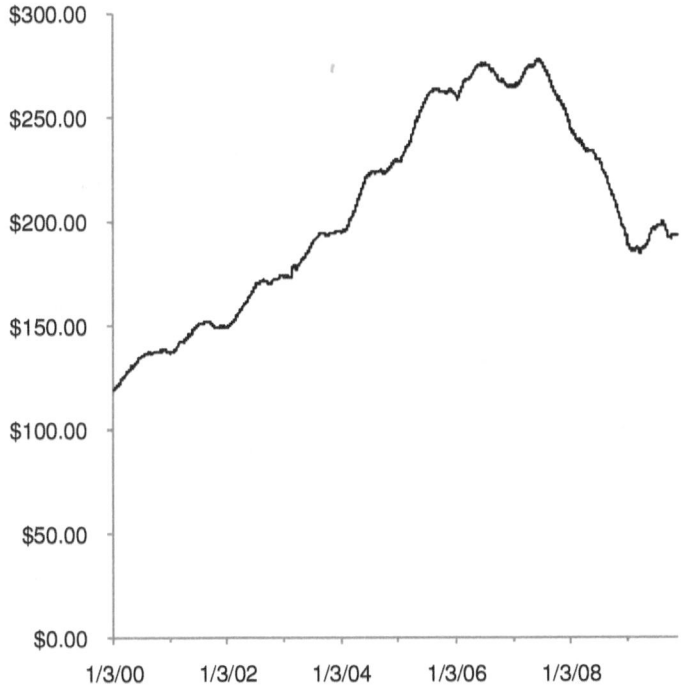

Figure 5.2-A, Radar Logic's RPX index for 25 MSA Composite – 28 day aggregate.

updated price distribution, the index is computed for the MSA. Utilizing this methodology, the index reveals repeating price patterns through the year that correlates with known "sales seasons". Additionally, the distribution curve is continually updating which reflects the current market.

Looking at the chart (See Figure 5.2-B), we can see that the property values in Boston and Chicago have a similar saw tooth pattern. Upon further examination, we find a seasonal

Synthetic Real Estate Investment

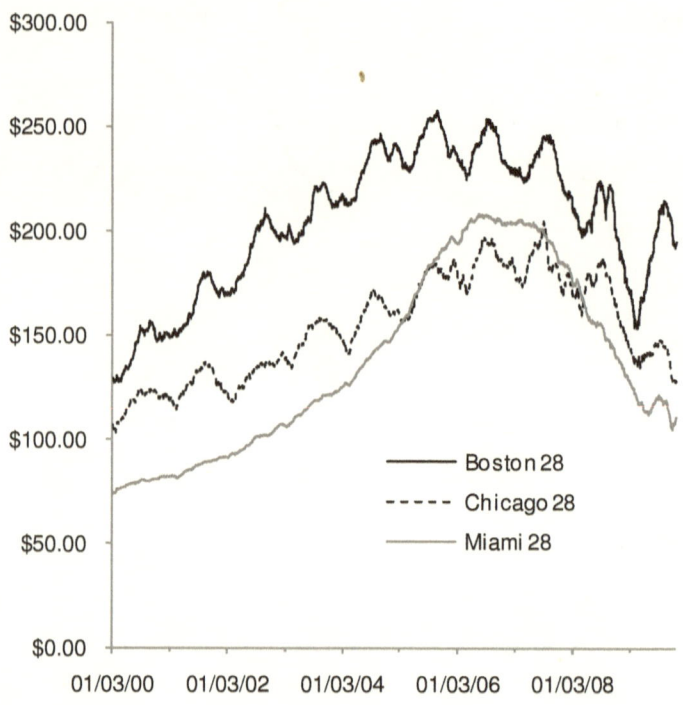

Figure 5.2-B, RPX 28 day aggregate indices for Miami, Boston, and Chicago.

factor at play. The peaks occur in the summer or warmer months, while the valleys are during the winter. Miami on the other hand, does not have winter weather. No such pattern can be seen. Clearly, weather has an impact on home sales values. It would seem winter weather reduces the number of buyers which reduces demand for homes. Could sellers be willing to take a lower price during winter months rather than hope for a buyer and higher price in warmer months?

The RPX composite index is a composite weighted index of the twenty-five constituent MSA's. After each MSA index is calculated, they are weighted based on per square foot price, building area, and number of transactions. Then the index is computed as the weighted average of the MSA's daily levels.

RPX trading is also done using swap agreements. The swaps are also similar in nature to forward contracts. Trades are done through brokers over the counter since there is not a market place to conduct trading. Contract notional values are still high with $2 million being considered a small deal. Again, this puts RPX derivatives out of range for the small investor – at least in the near term.

5.3 S&P / Case-Shiller

The S&P / Case-Shiller Home Price Indices are the results of many years of labor by Karl Case, Robert Shiller, and Allan Weiss. The indices track the value of single-family housing in twenty different U.S. metropolitan statistical areas (MSA). Two composite indices are also produced which track home values in ten MSA regions and twenty MSA regions. The major goal of the indices is to serve as reliable indicators of home prices. To meet that goal price changes are measured between similar quality homes. Because no two homes are ever truly alike, a repeat sales method was developed to measure price changes on a home which has been sold multiple times.

S&P-Case & Shiller Home Price Indices – MSA's Covered	
Included in Composite 10	
Boston	Chicago
Denver	Las Vegas
Los Angeles	Miami
New York	San Diego
San Francisco	Washington D.C.
Included in Composite 20	
Atlanta	Charlotte
Cleveland	Dallas
Detroit	Minneapolis
Phoenix	Portland
Seattle	Tampa

Table 5.3-A

The indices are published monthly with a two-month lag time for the data being reported. For example, in December they publish the report for the October index levels. To construct the index, each month data is collected from government databases for each MSA. Same home sales know as "sales pairs" are sought out. A sales pair is two sales of the same home. The last sale in the sales pair would occur (actually be recorded at the municipality) in

the month that we are collecting index data for. The prior sale could be any time in the past.

5.0 Real Estate Indices

To be included in the dataset the sales pair has to meet several requirements. First, the property has to be a single family home. Condominiums, small multifamily and other residential property types are excluded. The property needs to have sold once already which excludes newly constructed homes and pre-development home sales. All transactions are arms-length; no sales between family members or "sweet heart deals" are included. Finally, the transactions must be further than six months apart to filter out "flips" and redevelopment deals.

Why are so many transactions excluded? The indices are trying to measure changes in market price levels. In an effort to compare apples to apples, the data is limited to single-family homes that constitute the majority of the transaction data. Further filtering is done to strive to keep a constant quality for comparison. For instance, if a home undergoes significant renovations or a pool addition the price change in the sale would not be a good indicator for property value. The same house has essentially changed between sales – comparing apples to oranges. Any increase in value would probably be due to the homes structural changes.

After the sales pairs have been acquired and filtered, they are split into price tiers of low, medium, and high priced homes (See Figure 5.3-A). The tiers price levels are set by evenly dividing the number of sales pairs in each price level – if there are thirty sales pairs then the ten lowest priced are put in the low tier and so on. Only the first sale is

Synthetic Real Estate Investment

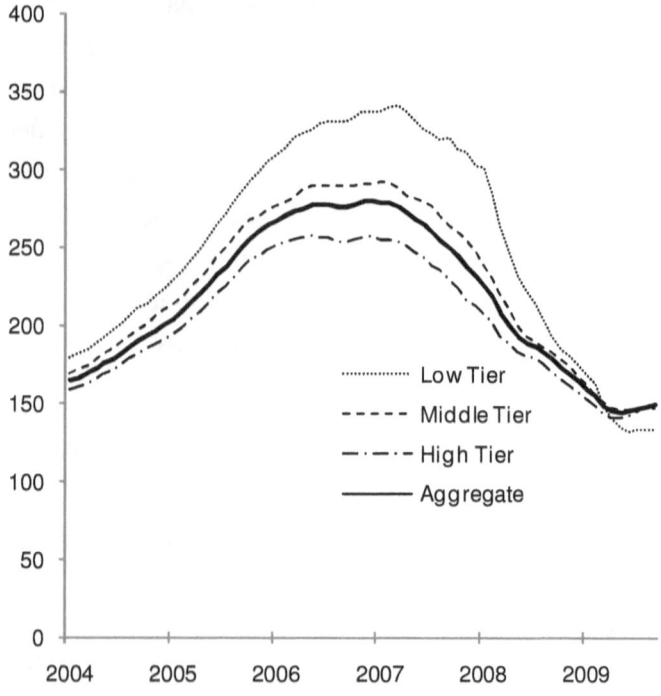

Figure 5.3-A, Miami Case-Shiller home value tiers.

considered for tiers. Since we are measuring the change in property value, the first value is our starting point. The second sale price will go to help define the change in property value. Over time, a property may be considered in different tiers merely due to the initial price and distribution of sales pairs. Different tiers of the market vary in price change and volume of sales as supply and demand move about. In fact, the lower tiered properties seem to appreciate in value better than higher value properties. The higher tiered homes tend to track the index due to the data weighing which occurs in the next step. Considering each tier separately helps the indices track housing value movement more precisely, helping to achieve the goal of a consistent benchmark.

Additional factors, know as weights, are now applied to our tiered groups. A mispricing weight is applied to sales pairs to help dampen the effect of very large movements in prices. Large price movements may be due to buyers paying too much, or a home that was severely neglected and bought at a large discount (a good flip candidate). Weights for the sales pair pricing starts at one and will always be greater than zero. The amount of down weighting will depend on the spread between the sales prices. Sale pair price changes are compared to the market price change. The greater the difference between the sales and market price changes, the greater the degree of down weighting for the sales pair. Typically, only 10-15% of all sales pairs in a region are weighted down due to price changes.

The next weight is considered for the time interval between the sales for each sales pair – an interval weight. It is reasonable to assume that the longer the time between sales periods the more likely that a renovation has been done to the house, or that the neighborhood has undergone changes. To account for this interval weights are applied to the sales pairs. The interval weights are determined from statistical models that measure the variance between transactions with respect to the time interval. For example, a sales pair with a

Synthetic Real Estate Investment

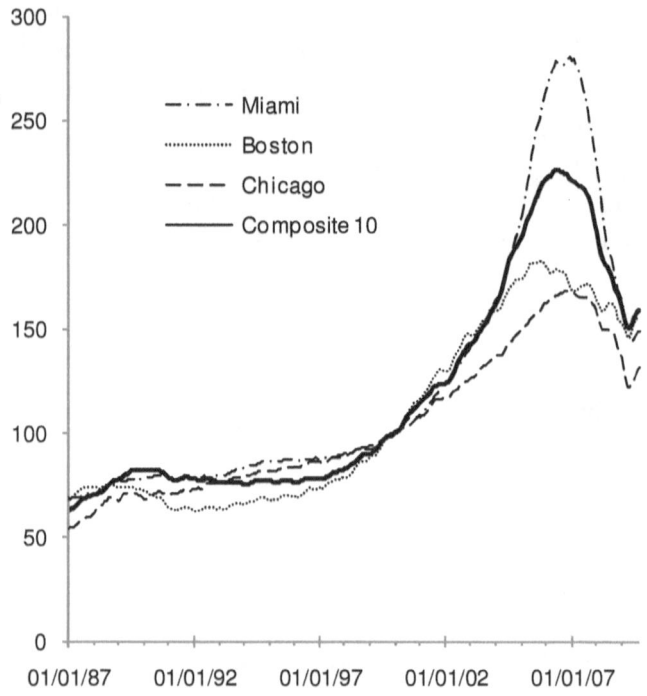

Figure 5.3-B, S&P/Case-Shiller Indices: Composite 10, Miami, Chicago, and Boston.

time interval of 10 years between sales would be weighed down around forty-five percent when compared to a home that had sold within a year.

From our filtered, sorted, and weighted sales pairs the index is computed. The index is computed monthly using the current and prior two-month periods for the calculations. A three-month moving data set, a moving average. Averaging offsets accuracy issues from the sales reporting delay to the counties. Additionally, it provides a

5.0 Real Estate Indices

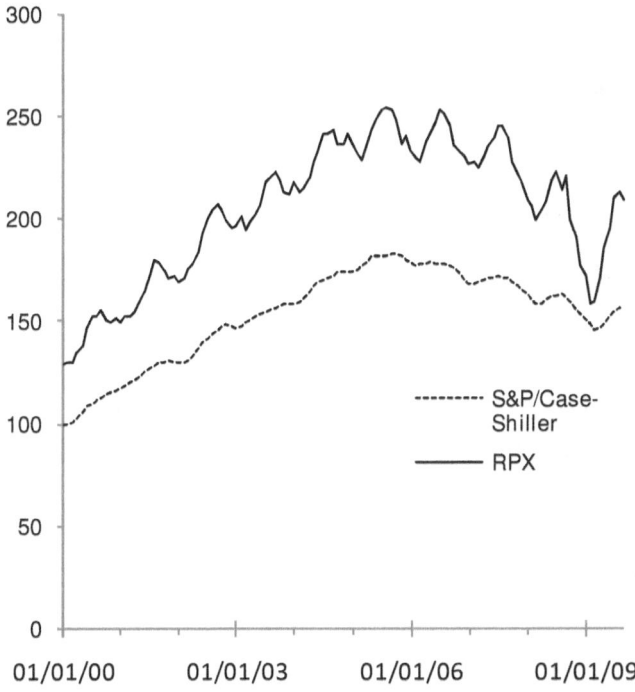

Figure 5.3-C, Boston Indices comparison.

large enough data set to extract better results. Finally, the composite indices are composed of the weighted constitute MSA indices based upon their total values in relation to the total group value. Back in the year 2000, all indices were set at a base value of 100. This time milestone also marks the point at which the computation methodology for the index was changed from a regression type model to a chain weighting procedure – what we have gone over.

Looking at the chart with Boston MSA data (See Figure 5.3-C), we can see that the S&P/Case-Shiller Indices are much smoother than Radar Logic's RPX. The averaging of three periods tends to smooth out the index. Comparing the RPX to Case-Shiller is not possible since Case-Shiller is an index of price levels – not an actual price, however, the values do seem to follow a similar path. In fact, the correlation between the two data sets is 0.97.

For trading, the S&P/Case-Shiller has a broad range of property derivatives types to trade. Actual futures contracts are available through the CME Group. Options are available on futures, but are rare and hard to come by. Currently, the S&P/Case-Shiller is the main index for trading in U.S. home values.

6.0 Property Derivatives

6.1 Swaps and Forwards

A swap is a contractual agreement in which one party will exchange the returns on a particular item for the returns of a different item from another party, the counterparty, for a specific time. In property derivatives, the swap generally comprises of the property returns of an index exchanged for a fixed rate (See Figure 6.1-A). The property returns are floating rates. Early on, a property index was trade against the prevailing fixed rate measure such as LIBOR or 10 year Treasuries. Investors went long a position by "purchasing" the floating rate in exchange for paying a fixed rate, or they may go short by "selling" the floating rate in return for the fixed rate. An investor who feels the market will improve generally takes a long position. A short position is an investor who believes the market will underperform relative to the index. Payments at the beginning of the contract are set up so that the payment to each party nets to zero. In addition, the total value of the swap (the notional amount) is not exchanged. Only the variations from the swaps fixed index rate require that funds exchange at predetermined time intervals.

Generally, the fixed rate payments were made quarterly at the three month LIBOR rate plus a spread. The floating rate payments were made annually based upon the percentage change in the property index chosen, generally the total property return index. Banks and brokerage houses would act as intermediaries matching counterparties to facilitate deals. Standard agreements were entered by both sides as to the terms of the deal.

Since 2008, the deal model has been simplified. The agreement has been modified to a forward contract. Banks and brokerage houses are acting as market makers allowing deals to execute quicker and reduce counterparty risk. The market pricing of the swaps is based on the expected percentage change in the index over the contract period and set by the market. Contracts are settled annually for both parties. Furthermore, a contract can be exited (unwound) at any time prior to the expiration date. There are still two

Figure 6.1-A, Swap agreement diagram

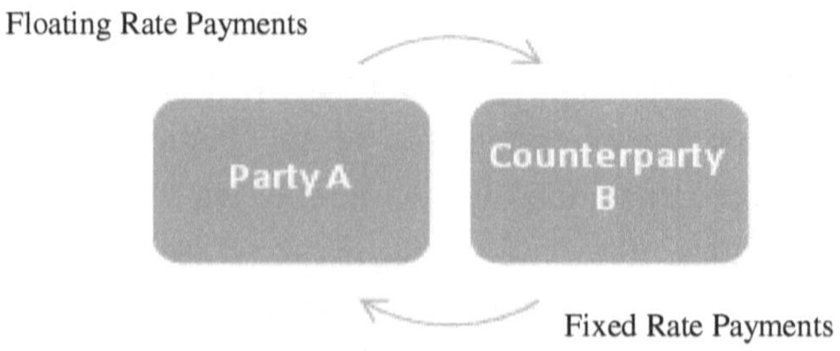

legs of the swap. The fixed leg is the percentage rate quoted, while the floating leg is the percentage change in the index from one year to the next. Contract maturities are yearly from one to five years. Table 6.1-A below illustrates how forwards are quoted in the market:

Index	Start Date	End Date	Fix Rate (%)
NCREIF NATIONAL 1Y	Dec-08	Dec-09	-17.53
NCREIF NATIONAL 2Y	Dec-08	Dec-10	-9.85
NCREIF NATIONAL 3Y	Dec-08	Dec-11	-7.0
NCREIF NATIONAL 4Y	Dec-08	Dec-12	-5.0
NCREIF NATIONAL 5Y	Dec-08	Dec-13	-3.0

Table 6.1-A, Property forward rates.

To illustrate how forwards may work, let us suppose we are looking to go long (pay a fixed rate to receive the floating rate) a three year contract which has a fixed mid rate of (-7) percent. The notional amount we are purchasing is $10 million. Therefore, we can calculate a fixed payment:

$$\$10,000,000 \times (-0.07) = (-\$700,000)$$

The contract is netted out to zero payment; so although we are to receive a payment, we are required to make a payment of the same amount (See Eq. 6.1-1). No principal is exchanged on the $10 million notional amount, but margin requirements need to be deposited.

$$Fixed\ Payment = -(Floating\ Payment) \quad \text{Eq. 6.1-1}$$

Let us assume that our long position in the forward performs as follows (See Table 6.1-B):

Year	Δ NCREIF[1]	Fixed Rate	Fixed Payment[2]	Floating Payment	Amount Due[3]
Dec 2009	-7%	-7%	$700,000	-$700,000	$0
Dec 2010	-10%	-7%	$700,000	-$1,000,000	-$300,000
Dec 2011	+3%	-7%	$700,000	-$300,000	$400,000

Table 6.1-B, 3 year forward contract results - long position.

The Amount Due is the amount that is either paid or received each year due to the yearly movement of the index in relation to the fixed rate. In the first year the change in the index matched the fixed rate, therefore, no payment is due to either party. In the second year (Dec 2010), the index was down from Dec 2009 by 10% that is 3% lower than the fixed payment. The investor who was long (receiving the index) would have to pay $300,000. Year three (Dec 2011) showed a positive gain in the index from Dec 2010 of 3%, therefore, the investor going long the index would receive a payment of $400,000.

---

[1] Year to year changes in the index value.
[2] We are receiving payment because the rate charged to go long was negative, so the value is positive. If the rate were positive, this value would be negative. We would make a payment.
[3] If negative, we must pay the amount. If positive, we receive the amount.

6.0 Property Derivatives

If we had gone short on the three year forward, our scenario would have looked as follows (See Table 6.1-C):

Year	Δ NCREIF	Fixed Payment	Floating Payment	Amount Due
Dec 2009	-7%	-$700,000	$700,000	$0
Dec 2010	-10%	-$700,000	$1,000,000	$300,000
Dec 2011	+3%	-$700,000	$300,000	-$400,000

Table 6.1-C, 3 year forward contract results - short position.

To summarize, the investor going long (buying the index) is expecting improving market conditions. The investor going short (selling the index for a fixed payment) is expecting deteriorating market conditions. Annually, the amount due each party is calculated based on that years change in the index. Both payments are netted out so only the amount due is based on the variance of the index change vs. the fixed rate.

These agreements allow investors to take on real estate risk through the index without having to deal with actual bricks and mortar – synthetic real estate. Investors are dealing with relative values of real estate measured by an index not with specific building and site issues. With indices covering various property types, trades have been done for specific property types such as residential, retail, and office. Within the residential indices, there are even specific cities (MSA's) and regions that trade. By trading real estate risk, a broad range of strategies can be deployed by the well-informed investor.

Unfortunately, the forward agreements have a major drawback for the small investor. They were primarily set up with large investors and institutions in mind. The average contract (notional) amount is around $5 million. Hundreds of thousands of dollars are required to set up agreements with the banks or brokers to conduct trading. You need to deposit 10-20% cash as collateral as well as the ability to cover and guarantee the entire contract value. Trading is done over the counter either through a broker or with a financial institution. They are out of reach for most small investors.

Where the forwards are valuable to us is they give us a window into what those in the market feel about the future, implied returns. Although we understand that it is impossible to predict what will happen in the future, the implied returns show the current future expectations of the market. Radar Logic publishes the implied home price appreciations on their website for the PRX index. Each month they update the implied home price appreciation (HPA) from the time of publication to the expiration of each contract. As the contract gets closer to expiration, the implied HPA will eventually converge to the closing price. Far from being perfect, the implied HPA is generally good at predicting the market's direction. It provides a good metric to measure our predictions and expectations.

6.2 Real Estate Futures

Futures are legally binding agreements between parties who each have specific obligations spelled out in the contract. The future agreement and commodity (index in our case) are standardized which allows traders to enter into and exit their positions. Trading is done through an exchange, which helps facilitate trades with market makers and clearinghouses. The main differences between futures and forwards are that futures are marked to market and guaranteed by the exchange or clearinghouse. Marked to market is simply settling the accounts of traders each day based on the closing value of the future. Value gains are credited and loses deducted from the trader account daily. Having the exchange / clearinghouse guarantee the contract reduces counter party risk – the risk the other party will not fulfill their obligations. The contracts are priced based upon an underlying index with all settlements made in cash. No actual real estate is ever exchanged. As the value of the index changes, the future contract's value will also change. Buyers anticipating a future increase in the index values purchase contracts – go long. Traders anticipating a decrease in the future index level sell contracts – go short.

Synthetic Real Estate Investment

CME Group's traded S&P-Case & Shiller Home Price Indices	
Composite 10	
Boston	Chicago
Denver	Las Vegas
Los Angeles	Miami
New York	San Diego
San Francisco	Washington D.C.

Table 6.2-A

Currently the CME Group, formally the Chicago Board of Trade and Chicago Mercantile Exchange, has real estate future contracts on the S&P / Case Shiller Home Price Indices. Contracts are available covering ten major metropolitan housing market indices and the ten city composite index. Additionally, contracts on price spreads between indices are also available.

The contract size is determined by multiplying $250 by the future contract's index level. To illustrate, if the future contract was bought at 100, the contract size would be $25,000. The actual value of the index itself is known as the spot price. The minimum index movement allowed is 0.2 that equates to $50 increments for contract value. The contract months for the contract vary depending on the length of the future contract. Contract lengths extend out up to 60 months in length. Contract months vary depending on how far out the expiration date is. Yearly contracts and contracts with no more than 18 months to expiration are listed on a quarterly cycle: February (G), May (K), August (Q), and November (X) - the letter in parenthesis is the month's symbol for the contract symbol. For contracts running nineteen to thirty-six months, the contract months are May (K) and November (X). Over thirty-six to sixty months, the contact month is November (X). All contracts expire on the last Tuesday of their respective month. The last trading day for the contracts is at 2:00 PM the day prior to expiration.

The contract's symbol is composed of the contract, month, and year. For example, the contract CUSG0 is broken down into CUS, G, and 0. CUS stands for the composite index, and G stands for the contract month of February. The zero at the end is the year, which in this case is 2010. Taken together, the symbol CUSG0 represents the Composite Index February 2010 contract.

Future Contract Symbol Components			
Contract MSA			
Boston	**BOS**	Miami	**MIA**
Chicago	**CHI**	New York	**NYM**
Denver	**DEN**	San Diego	**SDG**
Las Vegas	**LAV**	San Francisco	**SFR**
Los Angeles	**LAX**	Washington, D.C.	**WDC**
Composite 10	**CUS**		
Contract Month			
February	**G**	May	**K**
August	**Q**	November	**X**

Table 6.2-B

A confusing point for the contracts is due to how the S&P/Case-Shiller indices are published. On the last Tuesday of each month, the indices are published with a two-month lag. For instance, at the end of December the indices are released for data through October. Spot prices for each index are based on lagging data. Cash settlements of contracts at expiration are settled on the day the index is published. A contract expiring in May will be settled on the "just" published index values for March.

Future pricing reflects the market expectations in the future values of the index utilizing arbitrage arguments. Arbitrage is done by a trader utilizing pricing differentials between markets to make a riskless profit. For example, let us pretend that a trader observed that a product selling on two different markets had different prices – market A and B. Market A has the product priced lower. Our trader would take advantage of the situation by buying the lower priced product from Market A then immediately selling the product for a higher price on Market B. In our simple example, the trader has made a riskless profit; arbitrage. In transparent markets, the arbitrage opportunities do not last long. Other traders would take advantage of the price mismatching. Soon due to high demand, the product in Market A would increase in cost, simultaneously; due to the increase of supply, the product would lose value in Market B. Eventually and quickly, the arbitrage opportunity disappears. Our product has reached a new spot price based on the actions of the market – no more free lunch.

How does this apply to property futures? Here it gets a bit fuzzy. The S&P/Case-Shiller Home Price Indices are not traded, so there are no arbitrage opportunities between the index and the derivatives. Pricing in property futures is based on arbitrage in expectations. The current price of the future contract implies the current market forecast of the index level at the expiration date. If the underlying index is

Figure 6.2-A, Miami August 2008 future contract value plotted along with the Miami S&P/Case-Shiller Index.

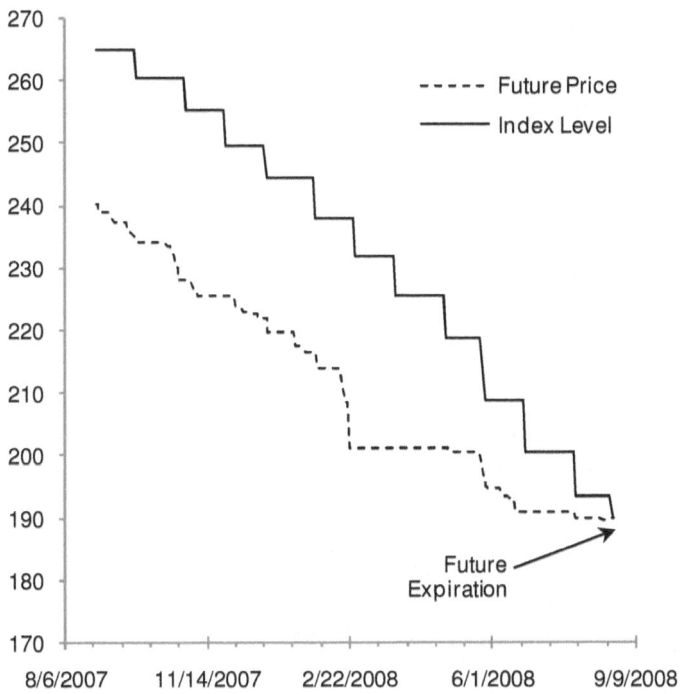

expected to decrease in value, the price of the future contract may be less than the current index level, discounted. When there is an expectation that the underlying index is going to rise, the price of the futures contract may be higher than the index level, a premium. In concept, markets are supposed to be highly efficient making arbitrage opportunities rare; "no free lunch". If the contract price paid happened to match the contract expiration price there would be no profits gained in contract value – the market had already priced the index movement.

Where profits can be made is when market expectations are off. As the future contract approaches expiration, the contract value converges with the index level. If the index is lower/higher than initially anticipated, traders who bought at the earlier price levels may realize a loss/gain. With property derivatives, there are really no arbitrage opportunities as might be found in currency or equity markets. The best we can do is to attempt to lock in an expected payoff.

Also seen in the chart for the Miami August 2008 (MIAQ08) contract (See Figure 6.2-A), initially there is a discount from the spot price of the index around ten percent. If you recall, August 2008 was the beginning of the sub-prime mortgage meltdown. The discount implies that the market feels the index should fall by ten percent from the current spot price of 264.89. As new information regarding the condition of housing and new index values

6.0 Property Derivatives

are published, we can see that the future price is continually adjusting trying to anticipate the index spot price at the contract expiration. When we get closer to the contract expiration, the future contract price will converge with the index's spot price. For this contract the settlement price and index spot price were 189.8. The value is twenty-eight percent lower than the initial index spot price of 264.89, and twenty-one percent lower than the initial future price of 240.2. It seems the initial market expectations were off by quite a bit. It should be noted that in the period before contract expiration that the future price may not track the index level as seen in the prior chart.

The chart for the Miami August 2006 contract is different from the August 2008 (See Figure 6.2-B). May 2006 was the first year that the property future contracts were trading. The first few months of future pricing were at a substantial premium. Housing prices in those days must have seemed as if they would go up forever. This belief was the prevailing emotion was at the time. If you had jumped in and purchased (went long) the Miami contract you would have lost money, even though the index spot price increased. The initial price drop was due to mispricing of the contracts by the initial market makers. As time passed, we see the future prices begin to track the index level. Still, the loss going long is due to expectations that the index will increase. It comes down to determining if the future contract's price, when you buy, matches your expectations for the index level.

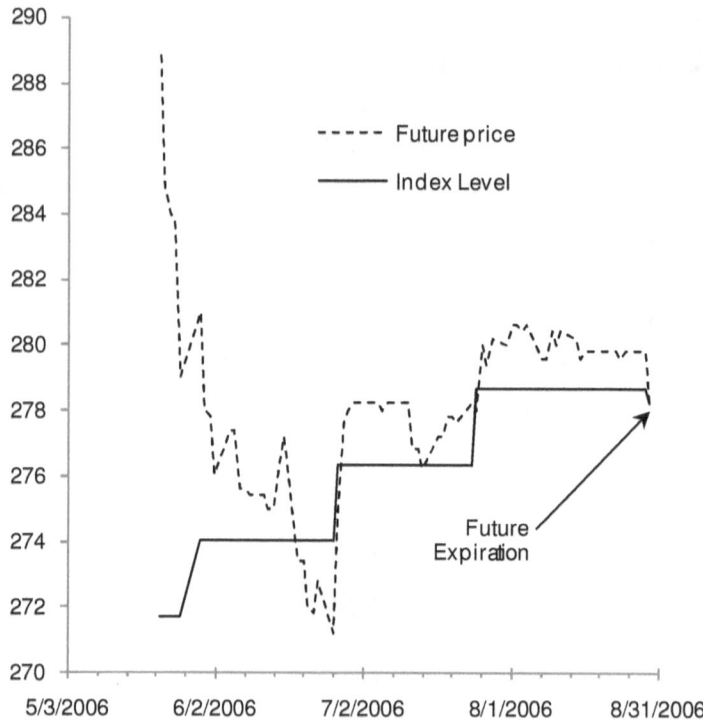

Figure 6.2-B, Miami 2006 future contract.

The future contracts that we have covered are known as outrights. Spreads are also available for trading. A spread is pretty much what the name implies, how far apart values are. The two types of spreads available for property futures are intra-market and inter-market spreads. An inter-market spread is speculating on the price difference between two different MSA contracts with various expiration periods. For example, a spread could be offered between the Boston February 2010 and Chicago November 2010 home price indices. The price of the spread is difference in expected expiration prices of the contracts. Intra-market spreads are also known as calendar spreads. Instead of speculating between different markets, we speculate on the difference in the expiration price of the same contracts in different periods. An example would be a calendar spread between a Boston August 2010 contract and a Boston November 2010 contract. Spreads have some advantages over outrights. First, the performance bond is much lower than an outright contract providing higher leverage for the same trade. Second, the structure of the spread is considered hedged, which is why the exchange requires a smaller bond.

Spreads are puzzlingly simple yet difficult to grasp. When looking for a spread trade we are actually trading two contracts, not one. One trade will always be long (hoping the index rises), while the other will always be short (hoping the index falls). For inter-market (calendar) spreads, the earliest dated contract is known as the front, while the later dated contract is known as the out. In inter-market trading of different home indices of the same date the first listed contract would be the front and the second listed contract would be the out, otherwise the earliest date is the front.

The out contract is considered a hedge for the front contract. If we take a short position in a spread, we are bearish on the front contract. Therefore, the front contract is short (short leg) while the out contract is long (long leg). We are betting the front contract will reduce in value relative to the out contract beyond the spread bid price.

Pricing for going short the spread is in the bid column of the CME Group webpage for the real estate futures. With a bullish or long spread position, we go long on the front contract and take a short position on the out contract. Here we expect the front contract to rise in value and the out contract to reduce in value. Again, the difference in value must be greater than the price of the forward spread – the asking price. To unwind a spread we need to acquire offsetting positions for both trades. Even if the long and short trades are profitable themselves, if the spread position costs more than the difference between the long and short legs we have lost money. Profitability is dependent on the spread price.

To illustrate, in March we take a long position on a Boston May/August contract. The May contract is at 100, and the August contract at 95. The current home price index for Boston is 105. The asking price for the long calendar spread is 8.0, which is greater than the price difference between the contracts. The May contract expires with the index and contact valued at 103. We have made a profit of 103-100 = 3 on the front or long leg. Now we need to close out our short leg. Prior to expiration, we can take an opposing position to close the contract, or we could choose to wait until expiration. There could be some margin issues if you continue past the front leg though. For this examples sake we must close our position when the front contract expires – we are able to purchase a long position at 92 that closes out the short position. Again we have made a profit of {95 – 93} two basis points, but for the short leg. Totaling the returns of the legs together, we have made a total return of five basis points. Unfortunately, we paid eight basis points for the deal – we would lose three basis points which equates to (3 x $250) = $ 750. We lost $750 when our individual trades would have made profits.

Trading of the S&P/Case-Shiller Home Value Indices is done electronically through CME Group. Any commodity brokerage firm or on-line futures trading platform with access to the CME Group can trade the real estate futures. Similar to other future contracts, the full amount of the contract is not settled until contract expiration. Only a margin requirement of 20% of the contract amount needs to be deposited into a trading account to take a position. The exchange has maintenance margins for each contract that allows a range of value movement prior to requiring more money to be deposited in the account to hold the position, known as a margin call. Fees for trading are inexpensive compared to physical real estate. Using a broker the total transaction fee for buying and selling (round-trip) a future contract is approximately $27 per contract regardless of the contract size. Electronic trading fees are only around $7 per contract round-trip. The fees amount less than 0.01% of the contract price, which is negligible.

6.3 Options

Options are contracts between parties that gives the buyer of the option the right to execute an agreed upon action within a defined timeframe for a cost. The main difference between options and futures/forwards is the buyer is not obligated to execute the contract – they have the right to execute for a fixed period.

In real property, real estate options have been in use for ages. Property investors would enter into an option contract with the owner of a site of interest. Typically a small fee is paid to the owner and the investor gains the right to purchase the site for the agreed upon amount within a set period. In these deals, the option contracts may contain similar details, but there are no industry wide standards. Each deal is unique. To sell the option for a profit the investor needs to locate a buyer and negotiate a sale. Executing the option is generally done to gain possession of the site, but some investors are successful at reselling them. Although a useful tool to the experienced real estate investors, they are not liquid enough for part time real estate speculators.

For small speculators an active options exchange is better suited. The Chicago Board Options Exchange is a good example. Utilizing electronic trading and clearing, a small speculator can enter and exit trades almost instantly through any on-line trading platform or broker. Unfortunately, at the time of writing, no property derivative

6.0 Property Derivatives

options are available through an exchange. Only over the counter options can be found, but in limited quantity geared toward institutional sized investors. However, due to the utility options bring to the table we should see market trading sometime in the future. Therefore, we will cover some basic concepts and issues to be found in property derivative options.

These days there are many types and styles of options. Property derivative options, however, seem to be limited to "vanilla" options – calls and puts. These options, similar to real estate options, are currently not standardized. However, they would all need to have some basic contract specifications. First is the type of option, a call or a put. Calls give the option holder the right to buy, and a put gives the option holder the right to sell. The next item to be agreed upon would be the quantity and index/future. A strike price is selected where the option holder can exercise the option. Finally, an expiration date and settlement terms are determined to include the current cost of the option. Most options are of two styles, European and American. A European option cannot be exercised until the expiration date – you are in to the end. American options can be exercised at any time during trading up to the expiration date.

How the put and call options work is straight forward. To illustrate, let us assume that a trader is interested in Miami residential property values. Looking at the available Miami future contracts, she calculates that the future prices are too

Synthetic Real Estate Investment

low in a contract that is one year from expiration. Let us assume the Miami housing price index being is at 149, the future contract being considered is selling at 140 – where the market expects the index level to be at expiration. Our trader is expecting a rebound this year, so she checks to see what call options are available. She finds a call option for a forward contract on the index with the same contract period as the underlying future contract she feels is mispriced. The strike price is 150 and it will cost $500. Feeling confident, she purchases the option. Because it is an American style option, she can exercise the option at any time the value of the underlying future contract exceeds the strike price, 150. To make a profit not only does the value of the future need to exceed 150, it needs to be high enough to account for the option cost and brokerage fees – around $520. Because we know the home price indices are priced at $250 times the index, she calculates to make money the future needs to exceed a price of 152.2. Since the index only moves in increments of 0.2, she had to round up.

A few months roll by and Miami is experiencing another boom – who knew? The price of the futures contract is now at 160, and our trader decides to exercise the option. She is able to purchase a forward contract at 150 and then sells it at 160. Her profit on the deal is $(160 - 152.2) \times \$250 = \$1,950$. If there were an active option market, the value of the option would have increased along with the future. She would have been able to sell the option itself for a profit. Had the value of the future not exceeded 150, the option would expire worthless. If she exercised the option under 152.2, she would realize a loss.

A put option is just the opposite of a call option. A put option allows the option holder to sell a futures contract at the strike price once the price of the future has fallen below the strike price. For example, if the Miami future was at 140 and we felt it was going to drop. We purchase a put option on the future with a strike price of 130 for $500. Including the option price and brokerage fees, $520, the future price needs to drop below 127.8 before we make a profit. The future and option expiration are the same. If the future price falls to 120, we would exercise the put option. We would purchase the underlying future at 120 and sell it at the strike price of 130. Our profit would be (127.8 − 120) x $250 = $1,950. If the value of the underlying future remained above 130, the option would expire worthless. Put options also change in value as the underlying contract value moves. Instead of exercising the put option, we could have just sold it − if there was a market.

Options are also used to hedge risk. Hedging is a way to limit losses for unexpected market movements. Think of it similar to auto insurance. We never expect to get into an accident, but if the unexpected happens we have insurance to help pay for the costs. To illustrate a hedge, suppose we were to purchase a forward futures contract expecting the price to rise. In order to protect our investment if the future price fell significantly, we could purchase a put option on the future. If we are correct in our estimates that the future price went up, we made a profit minus the cost of the option. In the event that the index plummeted along with our contract value, the option would limit our loss to the brokerage fees and difference between the future price and put option strike price. So if we bought a contract at 130 and a put option at a strike price of 120, when the contract expires at 110 our loss is (130 - 120) x $250 + (120 − 110) x $250 = $0. Considering the brokerage fees, we would have lost around $50. Similarly, when taking a short position, betting the market is going down, we can hedge using a call option. If the market goes up instead of down the call option gains would offset our losses in the future short position.

Options on real estate derivatives have some issues. First, there are not many options being offered so finding an option on a particular home index future is problematic. Without a market to trade the options they are over the counter, which literally means you must find someone and deal directly. Second, if an option is located we need to be sure that the price of the option in reasonable - here we run into some technical issues which make the pricing problematic. Current option pricing methodology does not work for options on the index since we cannot replicate the index. Options on the futures contracts can probably be modeled using a binomial model or Black-Scholes for the technically inclined. For the small investor, options on real estate futures may be a bit out of reach presently. Once a market in the property future options is up and running, the futures will become a useful investment tool.

Part 3

Applications & Strategies

"However beautiful the strategy, you should occasionally look at the results."

— *Winston Churchill*

7.0 Synthetic Market Exposure

Synthetic market exposure in real estate is taking on real estate market risk without purchasing a physical asset in that market. The market risk is acquired through property derivatives, which are based on an appropriate property index. If we were trading housing market risk, we would trade a residential index. For commercial market risk, we would trade a commercial real estate index. What makes our market exposure synthetic is that we are utilizing property derivatives to capitalize on property value changes in lieu of acquiring physical real estate assets.

Why would we choose synthetic market exposure over "real" real estate? Using the traded derivatives, we are not limited to our local market. For residential markets in the U.S., the CME Group has contract available for ten MSAs and a composite index. If you felt property values in the New York MSA were going to offer better growth than in the San Diego MSA, you would simply choose the New

York contract. Future contracts are standardized, while buildings are unique based on location and/or structure. The quoted future contract price is the current market value. With physical property, we must negotiate with the seller to come to an agreed upon sales price. In the following sections, it will be shown that a synthetic market exposure can generate the same real estate returns without the hassle.

7.1 Synthetic Flipping

Flipping a house is a speculative investment. A speculator buys a house with the aim of selling it at a higher price in the near future. Either the home price appreciation is anticipated to come from increasing home prices in the market, or the investment property was purchased at a discount from neighboring homes. If successful, a profit is made.

Synthetic flipping is also a speculative investment; however, we are only taking on market risk. Utilizing S&P / Case-Shiller Home Price Indices futures, speculators can capitalize from changes in real estate values. Instead of scouring the web and real estate listings looking for a specific house to buy, we look for traded markets where home values will move: up or down. With synthetic home flipping, we can make money in either a growing or falling housing market. We are not exposed to structural risk where a home needs more renovation than expected.

7.0 Synthetic Market Exposure

Management risks of buying too high or spending too much on décor are also reduced. Finally, we are not concerned about schools or neighborhoods.

Before jumping into technical issues, let us illustrate how a synthetic flip could be done. Ted wants to get into the residential real estate market. He works in technology and feels that the San Francisco housing market will see some increases. All of his friends are getting new jobs in the region, and he feels the area is going to spawn another tech-boom. Only problem is that Ted lives in Orlando, Florida. He considered trying to flip homes in and around Orlando, but the area has been hard hit by the economy. Orlando is expecting a slow recovery. The action is out West. Even if travel was not an issue, Ted now faces another hurdle. The average home price in the San Francisco region is $800,000. He only has around $10,000 to invest with. Therefore, Ted will utilize a synthetic flip.

Ted finds a futures contract on CME Groups website for San Francisco that expires in a year, contract SFRG1 (San Francisco, February 2011). The S&P/Case-Shiller index for San Francisco is at 135.81, while the contract is priced at 122.6. The contract is discounted by 11% indicating the market feels the index will decline, whereas Ted anticipates improvement. Noticing this, Ted digs more into housing values and sales for the region. After a bit more research, he feels confident that there will be some growth. If nothing else, he does not see the market dropping 11%. Ted calls his broker to take a long position. The SFRG1 contract size is 122.6 x $250 = $33,952. In order to make the trade the exchange requires that Ted post a bond of $2,025, which he does with his broker. The broker explains to Ted that if the contract value falls to around 100 he would get a margin call and would need to deposit more money. With the contract priced less than 100, the performance bond of $2,025 would be worth less than $1,500: the maintenance margin of the exchange. Feeling confident, Ted executes the trade. Unfortunately, we find he was wrong about the market. The housing index for San Francisco fell 8% to 124.9 from 135.81; however, the market had mispriced the future contract that settled at 124.9 from 122.6. From the contract settlement, Ted receives the difference between his contract price and the settlement price. His return on the trade is (124.9 – 122.6) x $250 = $575. After including round trip brokerage fees he is left with $548 for a return on investment of 27% on the $2,025 at risk.

If Ted had anticipated the San Francisco Index to fall lower than the futures price, he would take a short position. Taking a short position in the future contract is not the same as shorting stock. A broker does not deposit a large sum of money into our account as if we sold the contract. Instead, Ted deposits his performance bond of $2,025 and his contract obligates him to sell a contract at a certain price level at expiration, or close it by purchasing a long position in the same contract. To illustrate, the San Francisco home price index is at 135.81. The bid price for

7.0 Synthetic Market Exposure

the short position on a contract is low around 119. In order to make a profit the home pricing index would need to fall over 12%. This drop is higher than what is implied for a long position. Ted is cautious and double checks his research – San Francisco is in for a dramatic price decrease (he feels). He gets with his broker and executes a short contract position. Shortly after, his estimates of San Francisco home values prove correct. The home price index plummets; however, Ted still has a couple months left on the contract. Knowing when to take the money and run, he wants to take his profits by unwinding his position. To exit, he needs to purchase an opposing position for the same contract. A long position is available at 110 and Ted takes it. Because he has already posted a performance bond and is closing his position, the exchange does not require another deposit. The clearinghouse will match up his trades then clear and remove the positions. How did he do? For this trade his profit was (119 – 100) x $250 = $2,250. After fees, he earned around $2,220.

For a quick comparison, imagine he had purchased a physical property in San Francisco. He cannot afford the average $800,000 home so he finds a good deal on a studio for a sales price of $450,000. Somehow, he found $45,000 for the deposit. To entice Ted to buy the unit, the owner even paid the sales and closing costs. The location is good, and Ted feels he can sell it to some young IT professionals. For the example, suppose the condominium also lost 8% in value from the sale. Now, the S&P/Case-Shiller Home

Price index does not include condominiums, only repeat sales of single-family homes. Therefore, the decrease in value of the unit would generally not match the index, but condominiums can be more sensitive to the market. How did he do? Well with the decrease in value, the unit is now worth $414,000. If a buyer could be located, Ted would still need to pay some closing costs and a broker's fee. Each month a buyer is not located, Ted will pay an additional mortgage payment, utilities, and association fees. He may end up losing most of his deposit. Unlike a synthetic position, it is not possible to make money on physical residential properties when their values are decreasing.

Understanding that our example is not perfect, it does illustrate how standardization of future contracts makes life a bit easier. In futures, the price and "quality" are already known. Real estate has a wide range of prices and "quality". In order to get into the market with a physical asset, Ted had to compromise based on his ability to invest. Futures contracts are sized in smaller increments. The condominium unit at $450,000 would equate to roughly thirteen future contracts. Because of the smaller increments, Ted can deploy his investment capital more effectively. Suppose his research pointed to a rise in New York real estate prices. With the money sitting in the account he could take a position in New York home prices while keeping his contract in San Francisco. With physical assets, he would need to find additional cash and financing for around $300,000 for another small unit. In addition, he would now be floating $750,000 in debt if he could get the financing.

Now that we have seen an application of synthetic flipping and its advantages, let us look review the components of trading. First, the CME housing future contracts are limited to ten major MSA's and a composite weighted index of those MSA's. Although it may seem limiting at first, it becomes apparent that the indices do a good job of covering different regions of the country. Each MSA has different strengths and weaknesses, enough to keep it interesting. In the first part of the book, we reviewed home and property values. Putting the knowledge to work and conducting further research, we need to determine which of the ten MSA's has the best prospects for price movement – up or down. Econometric models on each region should be reviewed, which you can find on the web from venders, researchers, and associations. We are looking for employment, population, and income projections. Also, verify the average days on the market and inventory for home sales. If the days on the market and inventory are over three months, it could indicate a buyer's market. S&P/Case-Shiller Home Price Indices can be downloaded free at Standard & Poor's website. Once we feel comfortable with our research on a few MSA's, we can look at the future contracts. If that seems overwhelming, you can focus on just your favorite.

The future contracts can be viewed free at the CME Group website under the S&P/Case-Shiller Home Price Indices. Once on the pricing web pages, each contract can be viewed. The Contract Overview shows the expiration of the contract, symbol, and last price. In the next column we have the outrights, our main interest. Outright literally means to buy the contract "outright". Listed are the bid size, bid price, ask price, and ask size. The bid/ask size refers to the number of contracts available. The bid price is what someone is willing to pay for the contract, while the ask price is what someone will charge for it. Generally there is a gap between the bid/ask price which may include a premium. Next to the outrights is pricing for inter-market spreads and intra-market (calendar) spreads that we will cover later.

From the different contracts prices, we can see where the market is implying home index values to be at the contract expiration. Our task is to see if we agree with the implied prices based on our research. If we feel prices will be lower, we go short the contract based on the bid price – make sure you intend the index to go below what you pay, not the last bid price. If we feel prices are going up, we go long a contract based on the ask price. One issue we could run into is that there may be no trading in a particular contract. The market is still new, so trading in real estate futures is in its nascent stage. As the market grows and matures, we should see an improvement.

7.0 Synthetic Market Exposure

Before we can trade, we need to open a trading account with a brokerage firm and learn a few basics in future trading. Pending everything checks out and we are familiar with the ordering and selling processes, we can begin trading. As mentioned earlier, the future contract size is valued at $250 times the index. When purchasing futures we do not technically pay up front for the trade, we place a performance bond. The amount of the bond can be found on the CME Group website, and is roughly 6% of the contract value at the time of writing. Similar to real property, the futures utilize leverage for superior returns. Back on the CME Group webpage, we can find the maintenance margin. Listed under maintenance, the value represents how low your performance bond can be valued based on the contract prior to getting a margin call from your broker. Speaking of broker, we need to verify the brokerage fees so we can accurately calculate where the property index needs to pass so we can make a profit. Because the futures are marked to market, each day of trading our account will be credited or debited based on the daily closing contract price.

To close out our position prior to the contract expiration we need to offset our current position. If we had purchased four contracts that were long on San Francisco, to close the position we would purchase four short positions on the same contract. If we are short a contact, we would need to purchase a long position on the same contract. The exchange would then net out our positions and settle the cash due. If we choose to leave our position open until expiration, the contracts would be settled by the exchange based on the position and difference in our contract value and the underlying index.

Earlier we had seen pricing for intra-market (calendar) and inter-market spreads on the CME Group website. Calendar spreads are taking positions in the same contract with different dates. Inter-market spreads are taking positions between different index futures; the price spread between Boston and Chicago contracts. We could use outrights to construct our own spreads, but the traded spreads require a smaller performance bond. Let us use Ted one last time.

Ted exited his prior synthetic flip with a profit. Through some further research and conversations with some friends in Washington, D.C., he feels the residential property values there will grow in a few months. His friend who works at a federal agency has explained how the government was going to expand, again. This trade Ted wants to utilize a calendar spread. Currently the S&P/Case-Shiller Home Price Index for Washington, D.C. is at 179.1 as published in December 2009 (remember the index level published is lagging 2 months – the index level is for data through October 2009). The calendar spread that Ted is considering is for the February 2010 (WDCG0 @ 170, the front) and May 2010 (WDCK0 @ 165, the out) Washington D.C. contracts; the symbol is WEDG0-WDCK0. For the spread, the asking is priced at 20 for a long position, while the bid is at (-18) for a short position, (a negative price only means the out contract must be less than the front by 18). Ted is bullish so he goes long on the spread paying the asking price of 20. For the spread, the performance bond is only $878 with a maintenance margin requirement of $650. He now has two positions, a long position in the front contract (WDCG0) and a short position in the out (WDCK0). February rolls along and the front contract expires at the index level of 176. Ted has made a six point profit on the long leg, front. Unwinding the short leg, the out, he is able to purchase an opposing forward position in the WDCK0 contract for 162. On the short leg, he picked up another 3 points. All together Ted has been able to generate a nine-point return, too bad he paid 20 for it. His losses total $(20 - 9) \times \$250 = \$2,750$. The effects of leverage are easy to see in spreads, but it works to magnify gains and losses. If he had purchased a spread that was reasonably priced, his outcome may have been a superior gain compared to outrights.

Finally, we can offer contracts to trade on the exchange by naming the quantity and price you are willing to trade. There is no guarantee anyone will take the trade, but it allows us the ability to customize contracts - in theory.

7.2 Synthetic Rental Property

This section is to illustrate how property derivatives utilized with other financial instruments can mimic the financial performance of an income-producing asset. As with any representative construct, it will never match the original perfectly. Since only residential home price futures are available for small investors, we are again limited to the ten MSA's plus the composite index. As future markets develop, we would hope for commercial property index futures in order to take either straight synthetic exposure and develop commercial synthetic constructs.

Going back to Chapter 3, we found that the returns on residential rental property were composed of rental income and a capital gain from the sale of the property. The rental income after taxes and debt service is generally two percent of the total project costs, and around ten percent of the invested equity – both after taxes. In order to receive the ten percent of equity in potential rent, the investor needs to carry a ninety percent loan to value mortgage, a significant risk. The value of a property future is a bit difficult to estimate. At expiration, the futures are settled based on the difference between the underlying index and the contracts position and price. To take a future position, a performance bond must be posted. If the value of the bond were reduced, we would receive a margin call to recapitalize the bond. If the bond is not capitalized, the exchange can liquidate the position. Therefore, to compare "apples to apples" we will consider the performance bond as part of the total costs similar to a mortgage. Both the bond and mortgage are obligations. The capital gain in the property is the difference in value of the property's purchase and sales

7.0 Synthetic Market Exposure

price. To build our synthetic rental property we will need to replicate both the rental income returns and capital value.

First off, we need to determine how large an investment we would like to make. Next, we need to determine which MSA to place our synthetic property. Similar to synthetic flipping, we are really looking for contracts that will provide price movement. It does not matter if the index is rising or falling, we can make value gains with either direction. Although the S&P/Case-Shiller Home Price Indices exclude apartments, the movement in the index is highly correlated to the NCRIEF apartment index. The S&P/Case-Shiller will provide us with the ability to capitalize on real property value movement that we need. Finally, an investment that produces at least a two percent return would need to be located. There are an endless number of possibilities for the synthetic "rent". Depending on the world's financial condition, we can choose from dividend paying stocks, money market accounts, bonds, etc. It would be wise to consult with a licensed broker to make sure the investment is expected to perform close to our synthetic rent return requirements. Like a property owner, we will need to monitor our investment to make sure it is performing. Instead of evicting a bad tenant who does not pay rent, we change the income producing investment. Let us jump into an example.

For the example, we are going to construct a synthetic apartment building in the New York MSA. Our research has indicated that the Big Apple is ready for resurgence. To be flexible we will keep the contract lengths to no more than a year. We will look at outright contracts and spreads. Currently the S&P/Case-Shiller Home Price Index for New York is at 175.01. Since we are anticipating property values to increase, we will review the forward positions on the CME Group website for New York housing futures. The contract nearest to expiration is February 2010 priced at 173.2. The next contracts are price as follows: May 175.0, August 174.0, November 174.0, February (2011) 162.00. If we consider the contract prices as what the market implies the value of New York housing levels will be, it seems a gradual decline has been priced in the contracts. Either we have unique knowledge or our estimations are off. Back to study our data. We are going to forge ahead with the expectation that housing values will increase this year. Not being able to get a trade on the 2011, we will purchase the August at 174.0 and keep rolling our position as long as we wish to keep the synthetic apartment in play. To enter the long position on the August contract we need to supply a performance bond of $1,688 per the exchange that is done through a broker.

Our synthetic yearly rent requirements are two percent of the total investment. This simulates the cash to the owner after taxes and debt service. We would prefer to keep this portion of the synthetic construct liquid. For practical purposes, we may only be able to collect our income yearly depending on the tax issues of the investment. Our broker has found a municipal bond mutual fund that has been

7.0 Synthetic Market Exposure

generating six percent returns consistently. To determine our additional equity contribution to make the rent hurdle will require some simple algebra.

$$(Total\ Investment)\ 2\% = 6\%\ (X)$$

$$(\$1{,}688+X).02 = .06X$$

$$X = \$844$$

We may need to round-up in order to trade, but the $844 investment into the mutual fund will meet our requirements.

For $2532 plus some small fees, we have created a synthetic apartment with exposure to New York residential property values. Think of our construct at one synthetic unit. Depending on our risk appetite and investment capital, we could increase the number of units. How do we compare to the real world. At the time of writing, a nine-unit apartment building in Harlem was listed for $1,100,000 with a net operating income of $82,184. If we could obtain a 90% loan to value loan at six percent interest with a thirty-year amortization, the yearly payments would equal $71,220. The cash left over to disperse to the owner is $10,964. The ratio of the cash to total expenses is roughly 1%. Had we run a full analysis to include building depreciation we would probably see the cash to expense ratio closer to 2%.

Synthetic Real Estate Investment

The synthetic is by no means perfect. Again, this exercise was to demonstrate that we could construct synthetics to mimic real property. When a physical real estate investment is broken down to its basic components, we are left with a cash flow and capital value component.

8.0 Hedging

Hedging is the attempt to reduce exposure to risk from fluctuations in the market. Unlike many securities and futures, physical real estate assets cannot be perfectly hedged. Property derivatives are based on indices that tract specific types of property values for broad regions. The location and structural attributes of a specific property may not correlate well with the index. If the property is located far from the index, area there may be no correlation.

In physical real estate, it may not be practical to hedge the entire value of the property. Therefore, we will need to ascertain how much of the property's value is at risk and how much of that risk we are comfortable with carrying.

8.1 Hedging Real Estate

As mentioned, we can hedge a portion of the property's value that we feel is at risk. Larger institutional investors (also speculators) would utilize swaps and forwards to limit some of their market exposure. For the small investor/speculator, we can utilize the real estate futures with CME Group. Utilizing the future contracts, we can attempt to limit our loss in property values if the market drops. A future can also hedge against an upswing in market values. Since we have covered the mechanics of housing values and futures, we will move directly into some examples. First we will look at hedging against a down market, and follow with hedging against a rising market.

We are looking flip a house in Winter Garden, Florida. The house costs $110,000 in a neighborhood were similar homes had sold for $130,000. Instead of purchasing an existing home, we could also be looking to sell a new "spec" home for $130,000 with a total construction cost estimate of $110,000. Either way we are looking to capitalize on a property value gain between our costs and the sales price. Additionally, we are interested in hedging any unexpected drops in property value.

Winter Garden is located near Orlando, but the closest index that trades is Miami. Although both cities are in Florida, there is no guarantee that property values in one city will have anything to do with the other. We should probably limit our index comparisons to the MSA's if we are in the same state and the Composite-10. If we are not in the same state as one of the traded MSAs, we should stick with the Composite-10. Since we are looking to hedge market movement, we need to check if our market correlates with the selected indices and choose the "best

8.0 Hedging

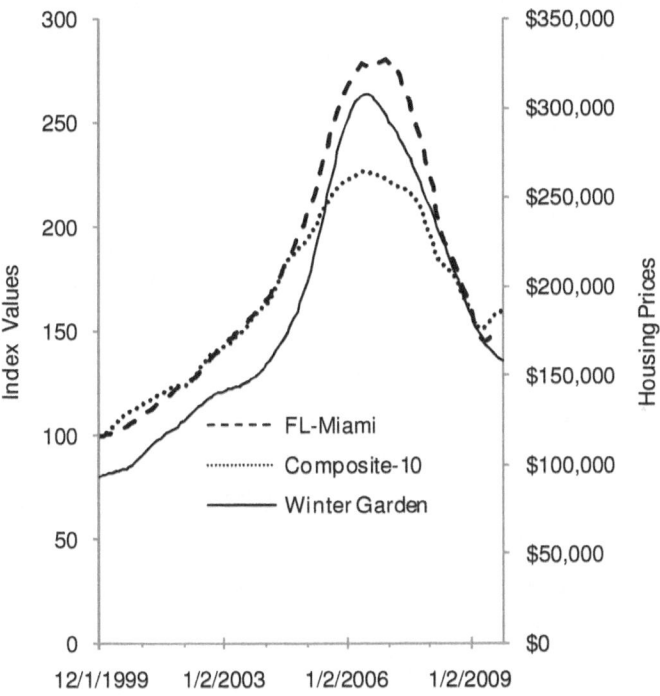

Figure 8.1-A, Chart comparing actual housing values to indices.

fit". A correlation implies that there is a relationship between the price movement of our house and the index. The analysis is simple and can be done on spreadsheet software. First, obtain some monthly data on our property's zip code or city for average home values. Today many real estate websites have regional transaction data that can be downloaded directly into a spreadsheet. Next, download the S&P/Case-Shiller Home Price Index from the Standard & Poor's website. They will give you all the monthly historical data for twenty-two indices. Since there are futures on only eleven of the indices, we must seek out the best fit from the smaller traded group. If you are lucky enough to be in one of the ten MSAs, you may still want to check how well the neighborhood prices correlate with the index.

When comparing the data, we are going to run into some technical issues. First, we are comparing residential transaction prices with a filtered repeat sale single-family price index. We are not comparing "apples to apples", but our purpose to find an index that is a reasonable representation of local home value movement. Next, none of the dates the values were published will likely match. Here we will need to make a judgment on how to line each set of data up against the other. For example, the Case-Shiller indices are published at the end of the month. Transactional data for Winter Garden is available, but is based on the 15th of the month – in the middle. Should we stagger the transaction data to match with the end of the month, or match it to the beginning of the month? Since the indices do not move too drastically each month it probably does not matter, but each case could be run to see if anything changes drastically in the correlation. Now we should plot our data on a chart to "eyeball" our property values compared to the indices of interest. The property values can be put on a secondary vertical axis so the data overlays correctly (See Figure 8.1-A).

The chart plots the Winter Garden transactional property values against the Miami and Composite 10 home price indices. Looking at our cart, we can see that data tend to move together reasonably well. The Miami index seems to be a better fit than the Composite 10 index, granted that Orlando and Miami are similar with heavily tourism based economies. Before we decide to utilize Miami index futures, one last step needs to be done. We are interested in comparing the monthly changes to each other to see how well the data matches for month-to-month changes. To do so, the following steps need to be taken with the data. First, in a separate column we will compute the log-returns. This is simply taking natural log (LN) of the current value divided by the prior value.

$$LR = LN(\frac{Value_t}{Value_{t-1}}) \qquad \text{Eq. 8.1-1}$$

Compute the log-return for each index considered and our local property value data. What we end up with is equivalently equal to the percentage change between the monthly values. If we place our returns on a chart, we can see how well each month compares to each data set (See Figure 8.1-B).

It is not as easy to "eyeball" a winner in the returns chart. Each index and our property values seem to agree in degree for major price movements, but looking close they seem to be all over the place. It is the correlation in the monthly log-return data that we are interested. Therefore, we can run a correlation calculation between our Winter Garden log-returns and each of the indices log-returns.

Synthetic Real Estate Investment

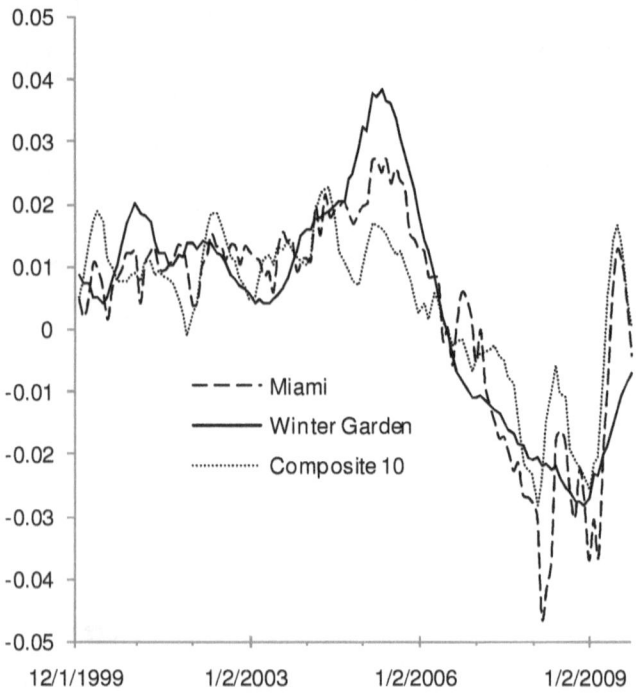

Figure 8.1-B, Log returns for housing prices and indices.

Log Return Correlation Coefficients			
	Winter Garden	Miami Index	Composite 10
Winter Garden	1.000	0.895	0.787
Miami Index	0.895	1.000	0.900
Composite 10	0.787	0.900	1.000

Table 8.1-A

The correlation coefficient ranges in value from +1.0 to (-1.0). A coefficient of one would be a perfect correlation of 100%, whereas, a coefficient of negative one would indicate the data is perfectly mirrored (when one chart moves up a point, the other moves down a point). The closer to one a coefficient is, the better the linear relationship between the data sets. A coefficient of zero means that no relationship is present. For real estate, we would be looking for correlation coefficients from zero to +1.0. Although there may be a situation where a negative correlation could exist between a property and an index, it is unlikely. So what does coefficient value need to be? He is the "rules of thumb". A weak relationship gives a value between zero and 0.3. Between 0.3 and 0.7, the relationship is moderate. From 0.7 to 1.0 the correlation coefficient indicates a high level of relationship between the data.

How did we do? Looking at the table with the correlation results (See Table 8.1-A), we can see that the Winter Garden log-returns have a high level of relationship with both the Miami and Composite-10 Case-Shiller Indices log-returns. The Miami index, however, is better correlated to Winter Garden than the Composite index. Therefore, we will look to utilize the Miami futures to hedge based upon the Miami index. Typically, another analysis would be done to test the hedge efficiency of the derivatives to the underlying, however; the property derivative markets are illiquid compared to other markets and the index cannot be replicated. We will need to run some numbers to figure out

Synthetic Real Estate Investment

our optimal hedge ratio of the project costs based upon our appetite of risk.

Going back to our Miami index log-returns, we will make a histogram with our spreadsheet to see the frequency of price movements in the data.

The histogram shows us some interesting information (*See* Figure 8.1-C). First, most of the price movement in the past has been positive, with 2% being the most common price increase. The highest monthly gains were at 3%. The losses

Figure 8.1-C, Miami S&P/Case-Shiller Index histogram of log returns.

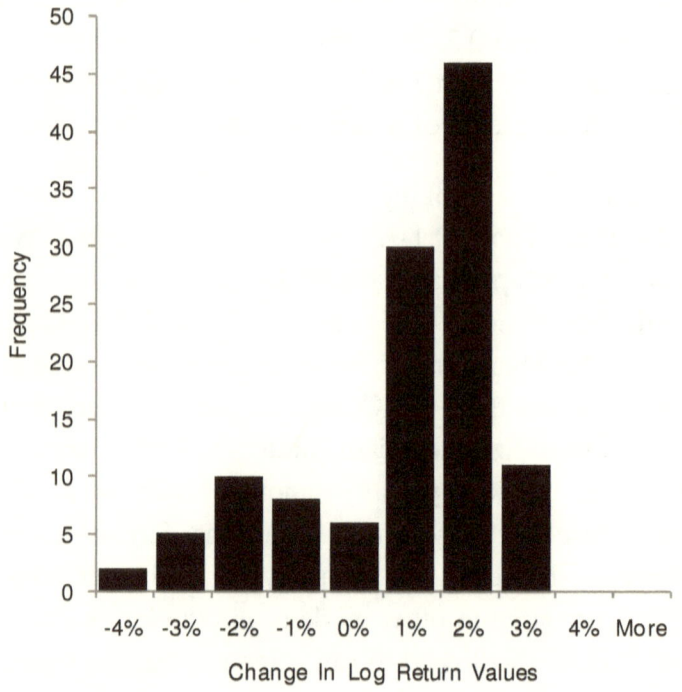

seem to have their own "typical" value around (-2%), with the highest losses at (-4%). We know the over speculation during the real estate bubble has played havoc with our chart, and the true distribution of prices is probably not as skewed as our histogram shows. It may be reasonable to remove the bubble, but this the exact behavior we are trying to hedge with/against – probably better to consider. On a more technical note, the log-return data is not distributed normally and is skewed to the left. The distribution may be a stable distribution. Briefly, this means is that if we utilize probability theories based on a normal distribution we will underestimate the probability of the higher market movements. To make life easy on ourselves, we will look at simply computing the worst, middle, and best cases. From scanning the results of our scenarios, we should get a good feel for what we are willing to pay for our hedge.

Which price movements should be considered? The percentage change per month is not too wide a range, from (-4%) to 3%. Therefore, to keep our calculations relatively simple we will look at four scenarios were the Miami housing price index moves by (-4%), (-2%), 0%, and 2% per month over our project life. The (-4%) monthly change is our apocalyptic scenario, while the ranges between -/+2% seem to be where we could expect to end up.

If we wish to be technical, we can compute some statistics for the Miami log returns. The mean computes to 0.003, which is effectively zero. With a standard deviation of

0.017, our returns would generally be between +/- 1.7%. Usually around two thirds of the data falls within the standard deviation. We could continue on assigning probabilities to index movements to determine what we wish to model. However, since the distribution is non-normal we would need to apply sophisticated analysis to the data to get reasonable results. Either approach of "eyeballing" or analysis can be equally effective. Even with the most rigorous analysis of past events, we still cannot predict the future any better.

It is time for us to research the prices of the Miami S&P/Case-Shiller Home Price Index (Miami) futures to see what is available. Before we begin, we are estimating our project to take no more than six months – eight months worst case. Therefore, we should be looking for contracts that will match our project timeline as best possible. It is the market risk during the project where we are most vulnerable. Looking back at the Miami futures, we find that there are some contracts available six months (May) out and nine months (August) out. The Miami index is currently at 149.09, the May contract is priced at 154 (ask) for a long position and 140 (bid) for a short position. The August contract is priced at 154 for a long position and 138 for a short position. If the prices were not to our liking we could always post a limit order at the price we are willing to accept. The biggest risk with the limit order is that it could go unfilled. In any event, we are interested in a short position since we are trying to protect ourselves from a downward movement in the market. Remember that a short position gains value as the market prices fall – similar to a put option. Upon reviewing the bid prices on the futures, it would seem the short positions are anticipating the index to decrease in value two basis points over a three month period, about 1.3% or 0.45% per month. Being optimistic about our project management prowess, we will settle on the six month contract (May). If the project begins to drag on, we can always take another position with the Miami futures. Additionally, we are picking up two basis points of index movement.

Now we need to run some calculations to see how much we should hedge our property to get to a level of risk that we are willing to accept. We will investigate three different levels to hedge: the required equity, the mortgage, and the expected sale value. Because the property is considered an "investment" property by the financial institution, we will be required to put 20% down. Again, the calculations are easily handled on a spreadsheet.

Synthetic Real Estate Investment

Winter Garden Residential Hedge

Total Cost	$ 110,000	Est. Sale	$ 130,000
Equity	$ 22,000	Future Bid (Short)	140.00
Mortgage	$ 88,000	Current Index	149.09

Hedge Positions

Value	Contracts	Cost	Notes
0	0	$ -	No Hedge
$ 22,000	1	$ 2,025	Equity Only
$ 88,000	3	$ 6,075	Mortgage Only
$130,000	4	$ 8,100	Total est. sale

Index & Property Value Projections

Monthly	6 Months	Home Sale	Contract Settle
2%	12%	$ 145,600	166.98
0%	0%	$ 130,000	149.09
-2%	-12%	$ 114,400	131.20
-4%	-24%	$ 98,800	113.31

Profit Projections

	Index & Property Value Projections			
Contracts	12%	0%	-12%	-24%
0	$ 35,600	$ 20,000	$ 4,400	$ (11,200)
1	$ 28,855	$ 17,728	$ 6,600	$ (4,527)
3	$ 15,364	$ 13,183	$ 11,001	$ 8,819
4	$ 8,619	$ 10,910	$ 13,201	$ 15,492

Returns

	Index & Property Value Projections			
Contracts	12%	0%	-12%	-24%
0	32%	18%	4%	-10%
1	26%	16%	6%	-4%
3	14%	12%	10%	8%
4	8%	10%	12%	14%

Table 8.1-B, Hedged home investment scenarios.

8.0 Hedging

Table 8.1-B shows the projected monthly index movements that we had ascertained from the log-return histogram. Continuing the index movement out for six months, the index change ranges from a 12% increase down to a 24% decrease. The value of the hedge represents "$ -"no hedge, the 20% equity, the mortgage, or the expected home sale value. To determine the number of futures contracts to purchase for the hedge, the "value to hedge" is divided by the future contract value based on the bid price (140 x $250). The fit is not perfect, so we end up rounding the number of future contracts up to cover the required value. Our estimated property sales price is based upon our expectations of the local market at each level of expected index change. If home values did not change, or changed very little, we would expect to get our sales price of $130,000; 0% index movement. Since the index is measuring housing value, any gain or loss in the index level would be reflected in the estimated sales price. The property value gain/loss is the "estimated property sale" minus the total cost of the project, $110,000. To determine the estimated future value of the index, the six-month index change was accounted for in the current index level at 149.09. The gains or losses on the future contracts would be the value difference between the bid price at 140 and the estimated future value. The value difference is then multiplied by $250. It is assumed that the future contracts would be held to expiration. Finally, the total gain/loss is determined by adding the property and future contracts gains/losses together. To make it easier to compare the results the "total gain/loss" was divided by the total costs of $110,000 to get a quick gage of profit or loss.

The example has been simplified a bit. We do not account for brokerage fees, closing costs, insurance, and finance payments. All of which would need to be modeled in the projects initial feasibility study that can now include hedging calculations. Albeit our example is simplified, it shows how hedging can work for us. The return on the house will probably fall between the +/-12% range. The implied housing return on the index expects our August contract in six-months to be 2 points below the current index level, which would equate to a (-1.4%) change. If the market is correct, we will end up closer to the zero percent change.

Looking at the "profit/loss" column we see that without a hedge we span the return range from a positive 32.4% down to a (-10.2%) loss. Bracketing our concerns to the +/-12% range, the profit/loss is between 32.4% and 4%. The futures market is putting us closer to our 0% projected index movement for an 18.2% profit – or just below. In all of the above cases, we still make a profit, except if housing values in Miami drop by around 16% (calculated – not in the chart). Below 16%, we begin to lose money. Remember, all of our calculations are approximate since the index is in Miami and the house is in Winter Garden. There is nothing to prevent our home in Winter Garden from dropping in value while the Miami index increases.

In every case, the hedged positions will reduce the gains if housing prices increase. There is a price to pay for protection – there are no free lunches. The concept behind a hedge is to limit losses for unexpected market moves, a downward price movement in our case. Scanning across the "profit/loss" column, we can see that the hedged house projects do indeed limit our losses when the index loses value. The single futures contract hedging our equity does lose money in the extreme case, but at half the magnitude of not having a hedge. A hedge against the mortgage value, with two contracts, returns a profit in every case. When we hedge the entire sales value with four futures contracts, we also profit in every case. However, hedging the entire sale reduces our profits by a significant percentage when the index remains the same or move upward. Which level of hedging is best?

The hedge cost cannot be financed in the house purchase; it is a speculative investment, not real estate. Cash must be available to place the futures performance bond, plus a bit to spare in case of a margin call. In each hedged position, a margin call for every contract would have been made if the index rose 12%. If we are tight on available capital, one contract may be our only option. If capital were available, hedging the mortgage value with three contracts would seem to make the most sense. Although we are giving up 6% of profits if the index remains flat, having a reasonable profit in almost every case we modeled is appealing. Far from being a guaranteed, "locking" in a profit may make more sense than taking the risk additional return.

Another point needs to be made. The contracts are settled at expiration unless we have closed our position early. If we will owe money on our contract positions, we will have to pay at settlement in cash. If we are expecting to get the cash to settle from the sale of the house, we should probably give ourselves a bit of wiggle room for the sale of our house and opt for a contract further out.

8.1.1 Hedging against increasing value

Hedging a project against a downward index movement makes sense for physical assets. To hedge against rising values would be beneficial for speculators looking to enter a market in the near future. Supposed we would like to purchase a "fixer-upper" in San Francisco, but cannot make the purchase for a few months. To protect our purchasing power we can purchase forward positions in the San Francisco futures. How large a position we take depends on our financial ability, but it would probably make the most since to cover the anticipated down payment. If property values continue up, the index should reflect it with rising values. Had we purchased the futures at an appropriate price, we should also see an increase in the value of the contracts. Ideally, we would have offset the increase in property value with the increase in value of the contracts. Our down payment should have grown in value to match the increases in the market. If property values decrease, our contracts should lose value in approximately the same proportion. Although we have lost the amount of down payment available, the properties of interest should have also lost value. The down payment value should still be sufficient.

9.0 Portfolio Management

Risk is the chance that our investment will not perform as intended. Why the investment underperformed could be due to an infinite number of possibilities from the mundane to the unimaginable. Some risk affects many different industries and has broad effects, such as rising interest rates. Some risks effect only one company, such as poor management.

The higher the risk - the higher the "expected" reward. Back when we looked at returns for speculative real estate, we saw that the risk we were taking on required a 20% return on the money invested. This is much higher than what is typically expected from the stock market, an average of 10%. The additional 10% premium is being required due to the higher risk for the specific real estate from high leverage, illiquidity, and management risk. Had we paid all cash for the real estate, the required return would only be around 8%. The higher the risk of an investment, the more return the market will require in order to receive any investment. This explains why investors are willing to receive less than 5% to invest in U.S. Treasuries. Being backed by the United States Government (and our tax dollars), they are as close to being a riskless asset as an investor can get.

To control our exposure to risk, we must diversify our portfolio of investments. The basic idea behind diversifying is that a loss in value in any single investment will not have such a large impact on a diverse portfolio. Intuitively we understand not to put all of our savings into one stock or one sector of the stock market, such as tech stocks. However, we have still not truly diversified our investment. Stocks tend to move with the market at least 65% of the time. Although there may be some diversification within the stock selection, we are still exposed to risks that would affect the entire stock market, known as beta risk. True diversification requires us to spread our investment capital outside the stock market into other markets such as bonds, cash, and real estate. The net effect is that higher risk investments are dampened with lower risk investments. We are trying to turn a roll-a-coaster into a merry-go-round.

9.1 Portfolio Theory

There have been numerous volumes of work done on portfolio theory. Here we are going to touch on the basics to illustrate how portfolio theory can work for us, the small investor. The essence of portfolio theory is allocating funds to investments that maximize returns while limiting the volatility (risk). It is up to the investor to determine the level of volatility they are willing to take for a given level of return. The higher the return, the higher the volatility (risk).

Volatility in an investment is measured from the standard deviation of historic returns. Technically the standard deviation is the square root of variance – a measure of dispersion of data around the mean (please reference a good statistics book). The higher the standard deviation, the more a value moves above and below the average value – higher risk. For example, Stock "A' with historic share values of $100, $75, $10, and $15 has an average of $50 with a standard deviation of $44.5. Stock "B" with historic share values of $60, $40, $45, and $55 also has an average of $50, however; the standard deviation is only $9.12. Although the average share values average the same, we can see that Stock "A" is over five times as volatile as Stock "B". Stock "A" is more risky. The same measure of volatility can be done for markets. The stock market has a volatility of about 15% with return expectations around 10%. Bonds have a volatility of 8% with a return expectation around 6%. Real estate fits in the middle with a volatility of 10% and an expected return of 9%. All of the market volatilities and returns depend on the period that they are measured. The best bet is to verify the volatilities and returns with major financial websites and see where the

Synthetic Real Estate Investment

consensus is. The expected returns and volatilities can change depending on the period under consideration.

Plotting the risk vs. reward on a chart for the stock, bond, and real estate markets (See Figure 9.1-A), we can see how each market compares to each other. Risk is plotted on the horizontal axis, while the reward labeled "expected returns" is plotted on the vertical axis. Each market is represented by a point on the graph. Stocks', being the highest risk and reward, is far to the upper right of the chart. Real estate is in the middle, with bonds at the bottom left of the chart.

Figure 9.1-A, Risk vs. reward chart.

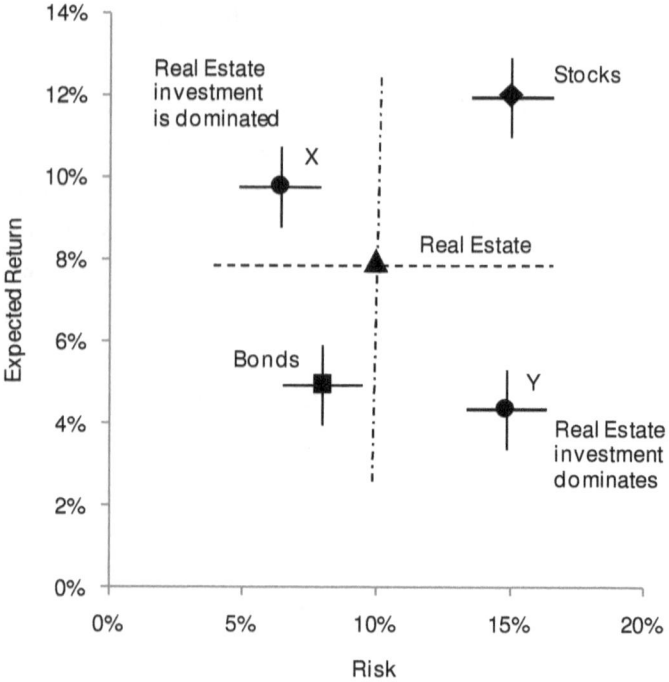

9.0 Portfolio Management

Plotting the potential investments gives us a quick way to select the better performing investments considering risk.

Suppose along with our stocks, bonds, and real estate we were considering two additional investment types X and Y. On the chart, we would draw vertical and horizontal axis through each point. Next, we look to see where the investments lie with relation to the axis we drew for each point. If another investment was in the upper right quadrant of the grid of the point we were looking at, the other investment dominates. An investment dominates another when it is producing a higher return at a lower risk. Any investment occurring in the lower right quadrant is being dominated – it produces a lower return for higher risk. To illustrate, let us look at our chart. After putting an axis on each point, we notice that bonds, real estate, X, and Y are a bit clumped together. We are only interested in dominant investments, so we begin by checking on bonds. No other points in the upper-left quadrant, therefore bonds are the best risk-reward point for its place on the chart. Now let us see how real estate is doing. We see that real estate is in the upper right quadrant of point Y, so it dominates Y. However, point X is in real estate's upper right quadrant. Point X is dominating real estate. We would choose investment X over real estate and investment Y. Stocks are the dominate investment over in the upper right region of the chart. From the group of investments being considered we would choose to invest in bonds, investment X, and stocks.

9.1.1 Portfolio Allocation

Now that we know what we are investing in, we need to determine how much money to place into each investment – our portfolio allocations. Generally, we are looking to maximize our return for our chosen level of risk/volatility. Furthermore, we want to choose portfolios that are not dominated by any other combinations (portfolios) of the same assets. Let us consider a portfolio of stocks, bonds, and real estate (housing futures). The expected returns and volatility for each is listed in Table 9.1-A.

Investments in the Portfolio		
	Return	**Volatility**
Cash	4.00%	0.00%
Bond Fund	8.00%	8.0%
Housing	9.00%	10.0%
Stock Fund	12.12%	15.0%

Table 9.1-A

For each investment, we have the expected return and the volatility. We then need to enter the correlation coefficient between the investments. The correlation coefficient is the measure of how well the investments move together over a period with a value ranging from 1.0 to (-1.0); +/- 100%. The higher the correlation the more the investments move together in unison. A lower coefficient would mean the investments are less likely to move to together. To diversify we would like to choose investments with low correlation coefficients. We could compute the correlations ourselves, but it is probably best to see and use what the major financial institutions and websites are using. The correlations change over time and from period to period, so we need to verify the values every few months to be safe.

Correlation Between Investments			
	Stocks	**Bonds**	**Housing**
Stocks	100%	50%	25%
Bonds	50%	100%	0%
Housing	25%	0%	100%

Table 9.1-B

We set up the correlation table (See Table 9.1-B) to help us in the next couple of steps to determine the optimum portfolios. From the correlation table we can see that stocks, bonds, and real estate are 100% correlated with themselves – easy enough. Stocks and bonds have a coefficient of 50%, so they move together about a half of the time. Real estate and stocks have a very low correlation of 25%. Real estate and bonds generally not very

Synthetic Real Estate Investment

correlated, so we plug in 0%[4]. Now we compute the covariance between the variables as in Table 9.1-C.

Covariance Expectations

	Stocks	Bonds	Real Estate
Stocks	0.02250	0.00600	0.00375
Bonds	0.00600	0.00640	0.00000
Real Estate	0.00375	0.00000	0.01000

Table 9.1-C

The covariance measures how well the investments move together over a certain period. More importantly, the joint movement is considered the risk that cannot be diversified away, systematic risk. We will compute the covariance from the correlation coefficients using the formula:

$$COV_{ij} = C_{ij}\sigma_i\sigma_j \qquad \text{Eq. 9.1-1}$$

COV_{ij} is the covariance, and C_{ij} is the correlation coefficient. Sigma, s is the standard deviation for the asset also known at the volatility that we plugged into our chart earlier. To compute the covariance in the table, it is easier

---

[4] Correlations between investments change depending on the period under consideration. The example has been set up with values that may not correspond to current ratios.

9.0 Portfolio Management

to think of the data as if we are comparing two different instances of investment for each value. For example, to compute the stock covariance of 0.0225, the calculation is, $COV_{ij} = (1.00)(.15)(.15)$. The correlation of a stock to a stock is 100%. Since we are "comparing" two stocks, each would have a volatility of 15%. Other covariance calculations are more straightforward. Between stocks and bonds, the variance is computed by, $COV_{ij} = (0.5)(.15)(.08)$ for the table value of .006. All the combinations of investments have their coefficients computed, then complied into a table as previously shown.

On the chart in Figure 9.1-B, we see our investments plotted as points on the risk-reward chart. Additionally we see curves between our investment points. The curves represent a portfolio between the two assets. For example, the curve between bonds and real estate represents a portfolio of 100% bonds at the bond point. As we trace up the curve toward the real estate point, the portfolio is reducing the amount of bonds and increasing the amount of real estate investment. Once we reach the real estate point, the portfolio consists of 100% real estate investments. What the curves show is that a combination of assets can provide a return that is higher than the least risky asset, but lower than the most risky asset. On the bond-real estate curve, we see that the Y-axis values for return are always greater than bonds, and always less than real estate. Most importantly, the curve also shows that a combination of the

Synthetic Real Estate Investment

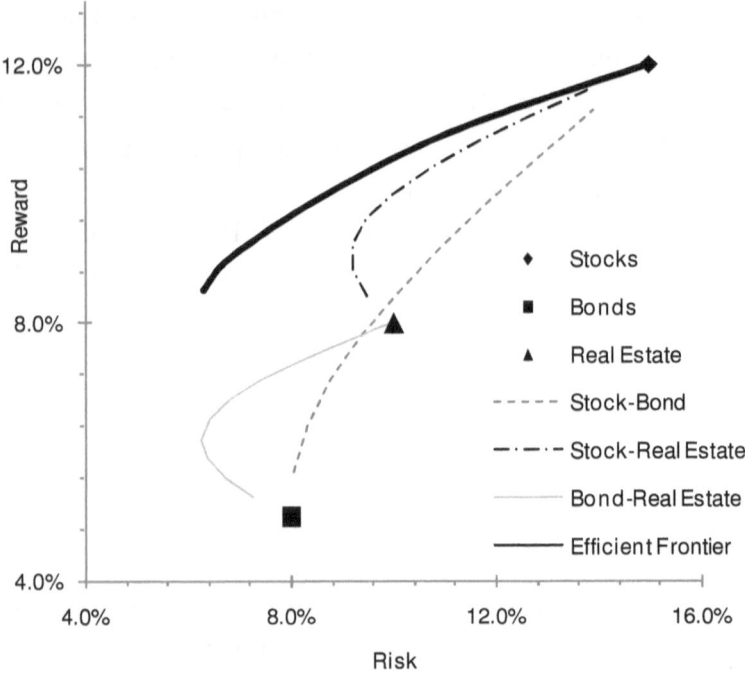

Figure 9.1-B, Efficient frontier.

investments can also be less risky than the individual investments. In the case of a portfolio of bonds and stocks, it seems the risk behaves similar to reward – always in between the original investments. Remembering that lines are composed of points of data, any curve that is in the upper right quadrant of a point we are considering on another curve is dominant. Similar to our pick of investments, we desire that our portfolio composition of investments be the dominant portfolio at the level of risk we choose. The portfolio should have the highest return for the lowest volatility (risk). This is the goal of mean-variance portfolio theory (MPT). Taking into consideration how each investment behaves (volatility) and relates to each other (covariance), we solve for the dominant portfolio. Utilizing the MPT, we can compute the risk of the "optimized" portfolio at each level of "expected" return. If we plotted the results, we would end up with the efficient frontier as plotted on our chart. The efficient frontier represents the risk-reward curve of the dominant portfolios. Looking at the curve, we notice that along the efficient frontier we obtain superior returns at a lower risk than the individual investments. In addition, a portfolio composed of all three of the investments dominates the portfolios consisting of just two of the investments.

To solve for the portfolio allocation using MPT, we are going to need a solver that solves will run the computations until it can find the answer (if there is one). Most spreadsheet software has a solver included or that can be easily installed if they were not part of the original installation. In order to help our solver to calculate results, we need to set up a few items.

First, we need to put in some "dummy" variables for the allocation of each investment. Next, the weighted covariance for each investment pair needs to be solved. The weighted variance takes into account how much the investments move together, but in relation to how much of each investment is made. To compute the weighted covariance we multiply the covariance by the amount of the investment bought in each category. For example, the weighted covariance for stock and real estate in the table is 0.000613. It is found by multiplying the covariance (0.00375) between stocks (39.7%) and real estate (41%) by their allocations. When determining the weighted covariance between an investment and itself (i.e. stock-stock, bond-bond, etc.), we must square the value of the allocation. In order to compute the weighted covariance for the stock-stock relationship (0.003546), the computation is (39.7%) x (39.7%) x (0.0225). With our weighted covariance chart set up, we can solve for the portfolio's risk. The variance of the portfolio is simply the sum of all of the weighted covariance pairs. To compute the risk we take the square root of the variance, which is also the standard deviation of the portfolio. The last computation we need to set up is the portfolio return. To calculate the return, we take each of the investment allocations, multiply them by their expected return, and then sum them up. With all of our computations in place, we can turn to using the solver.

Our goal is to determine the investment allocations to meet our required return at the lowest risk. To do so we need to set up the goals and constraints for the solver. First, we want the minimum risk value – set the solver to find the minimum. The variables the solver will manipulate will be our allocations to stocks, bonds, and real estate. Now we need to apply appropriate constraints. The solver needs to make sure our allocations in all investments add up to

100%. The allocations in each investment must be less than 100% and greater than zero (you could have negative allocations that represent short positions). Otherwise, the allocations will be greater than 100% and perhaps negative. Finally, our calculated return for the portfolio needs to match the required return. When we run the solver, it should produce a reasonable allocation of investments (See Figure 9.1-C). Be aware that not all levels of return will have an answer – we can only make as much as the highest returning investment. If we run several iterations and plot the results on a graph of risk verses reward, we end up with the efficient frontier.

Portfolio Allocation - Variance Minimizing

Req'd Return:	10.00%			
Calc. Return:	10.00%			

	Stocks	Bonds	Real Estate	
Expected Return	12%	8%	9%	
Volatility	15%	8%	10%	
Allocation	39.70%	19.10%	41%	100.00%

Correlation

	Stocks	Bonds	Real Estate
Stocks	100%	50%	25%
Bonds	50%	100%	0%
Real Estate	25%	0%	100%

Covariance

	Stocks	Bonds	Real Estate
Stocks	0.02250	0.00600	0.00375
Bonds	0.00600	0.00640	0.00000
Real Estate	0.00375	0.00000	0.01000

Weighted Covariances

	Stocks	Bonds	Real Estate
Stocks	0.003546	0.000455	0.000613
Bonds	0.000455	0.000233	0.000000
Real Estate	0.000613	0.000000	0.001698

Risk	8.73%

Figure 9.1-C, Portfolio allocation results utilizing variance (risk) minimizing.

9.1.2 Sharpe-Maximizing Portfolio

The MPT is a useful tool for considering investment allocations within our portfolio, however; there are a few drawbacks. First, we have to determine our desired level of return, which is based on our appetite for risk. Aggressive investors are willing to take higher risks for higher returns. A conservative investor is willing to take less return in order to reduce risk. Next, a riskless asset such as T-bills or cash cannot be used in our model. Any riskless asset is assumed to have zero risk (volatility). Researchers found that when including a riskless asset the efficient frontier would change. Effectively the "new" efficient frontier would go from the riskless return rate to a point of tangency on the efficient frontier. The point of tangency represented the optimal allocation of riskless and risky assets. Instead of worrying about investor preferences, the optimal portfolio allocation only depended on the expected returns. The investor could then raise or lower the portfolios return (and risk) by either lending or borrowing in the riskless asset.

For our purposes we probably are not able to borrow or lend large sums of cash, however; the inclusion of a riskless asset is important. It allows us to determine the optimal portfolio allocations, which would dominate over the efficient frontier we had computed. Requiring a dominant portfolio, we need to determine the optimal portfolio at the point of tangency. To do this we will utilize

Sharpe-maximizing portfolio, which utilizes the Sharpe ratio.

The Sharpe ratio is the risk premium of an investment divided by its volatility. The risk premium is an investments return over the riskless investment – usually cash or treasuries.

$$Sharpe\ Ratio = \frac{expected\ investment's\ return - riskless\ rate}{expected\ investment's\ volatility}$$

Eq. 9.1-2

The ratio is a good measure of risk-adjusted return. The higher the ratio computed, better the investments return relative to its risk and the riskless investment. A lower ratio would mean we are being inefficient, receiving less return relative to the risk. For allocating our funds into different investments, we begin with our prior setup for calculating the mean-variance. A riskless asset is added to our possible allocations. Next, we calculate the Sharpe ratio for each return. Instead of trying to allocate investments to mean a desired return goal, we use the solver to maximize the Sharpe ratio. We want to get the highest return per the risk. Let us look at an example.

Jane has $30,000 to invest. Understanding the importance of diversifying her investments she looks to put money into different asset classes; stocks, bonds, real estate, and cash. Speaking to her friendly stockbroker for consultation, she has decided to utilize mutual funds that specialize in stocks and bonds in lieu of a direct investment. For her real estate exposure, she will compare REITs with the housing futures. Actual real estate assets are not considered since she does not want to incur another mortgage. Any cash would be put into her bank account or another higher interest account.

After plotting the stock and bond funds on a chart, she eliminated the dominated investments down to one stock fund and one bond fund. Now she had to consider whether to utilize property derivatives or a REIT – real estate investment trust. REIT's are corporations or trusts that buy, sell, and manage income-producing properties. Many of the REIT's trade on the stock market and offer the investor the benefit of liquidity. Using a REIT stock, our exposure to real estate is through the decisions and actions of the REIT management. We are effectively investing in a real estate company. If the REIT makes poor management decisions or market sentiment is negative, the stock value can suffer. In fact, REITs correlate with stocks about 64% of the time. Compared to REITs, Property derivates are illiquid due to a low volume of trading. Sue is not looking to trade thousands of contracts, so it is not too big a concern. Since derivative pricing is based on the S&P/Case-Shiller indices, the derivatives reflect the true movements in actual real estate value. Home prices correlate less than 25% of the time with stocks. If Jane wants market diversification in her portfolio, she would be better off with the property derivatives – which she does.

Synthetic Real Estate Investment

Sharpe-Maximizing Portfolio

Investment: $ 30,000

	Return	Volatility	Sharpe	Allocation		
Cash	4.00%	0.00%		25.1%	$	7,540
Bond Fund	8.00%	8.0%	0.50	31.3%	$	9,377
Housing	9.00%	10.0%	0.50	24.2%	$	7,270
Stock Fund	12.12%	15.0%	0.54	19.4%	$	5,812
Portfolio	8.04%		0.73	100.0%	$	30,000

<u>Correlation</u>

	Stocks	Bonds	Housing
Stocks	100.0%	23.0%	25.0%
Bonds	23.0%	100.0%	25.0%
Housing	25.0%	25.0%	100.0%

<u>Covariance</u>

	Stocks	Bonds	Housing
Stocks	0.02250	0.00276	0.00375
Bonds	0.00276	0.00640	0.00200
Housing	0.00375	0.00200	0.01000

<u>Weighted Covariances</u>

	Stocks	Bonds	Housing
Stocks	0.000845	0.000167	0.000176
Bonds	0.000167	0.000625	0.000152
Housing	0.000176	0.000152	0.000587

Volatility   5.52%

Figure 9.1-D, Sharpe-maximizing portfolio calculation sheet and results.

9.0 Portfolio Management

The figure shows Jane's calculations and results. Based on research, she had to decide on what the expected returns would be for each category. Although not perfect, Jane figured the long running average returns would be safe. The volatilities also were based on longer-term information. Due to the housing bubble, credit crunch, and market crash (if that were not enough) the recent volatilities were very high - upwards of thirty-five percent. Feeling that the bubble was not likely to occur again in the next few months, she used the long-term volatilities. The only bit of information she had revised from our earlier example were the correlations, specifically between stocks and bonds.

Jane set up the solver to maximize the Sharpe ratio for the portfolio (See Figure 9.1-D). To do so the solver would change the allocations of each investment, including the cash. The constraints needed to be added to get a reasonable answer. First, since we were not going use large short positions, the allocations had to be greater than zero. Next, the allocations also had to be less than one (100%). Finally, the total of all the allocations had to add up to 100%. The solver would determine the maximum Sharpe ratio for the portfolio. Based on the allocation results, Jane would have a portfolio with a return of 8.00% expected with a volatility of 5.52%. The portfolio's Sharpe ratio calculates out to 0.73, which is greater than the bonds, housing, or stocks alone. For a higher return Jane would reduce the amount of cash, for a lower volatility she would increase it. This can be done through the solver. The other allocations move around a bit, but the cash position seems to drive the return changes. Now Jane can go to her broker with her allocations and work out how to put the actual portfolio together.

As we have seen, using portfolio theory, we are able to build a portfolio that meets our return and risk requirements. Although our calculations are far from any guarantee of being correct, we have a way to measure how our investments affect our perceived outcomes. Just remember to dominate.

Afterword

We have covered a large amount of information from urban economics to portfolio theory. With a reasonable level of understanding of housing values, the index, and property derivatives, you should be able to utilize synthetic real estate in your overall investment strategy.

Currently, the CME Group's S&P/Case-Shiller Home Price Index futures have been trading very lightly. The actual market for the futures has only been around for two years. As investors begin to learn how to utilize the futures, the market should expand. I hope that we could one day see contracts available for all twenty MSA Case-Shiller indices. In addition, development of commercial property futures is in the nascent stage. One day we may be able to take a position in a specific real estate segment in a specific MSA. Perhaps we will be able to buy and sell hotel futures in Miami, or flip synthetic office buildings in New York. The opportunities are endless.

As always, the reader is cautioned that these investment strategies are risky. Please do your homework. Do your best to avoid emotional projections of the housing market. As I myself have been a victim, we tend to rationalize our decisions and interpret data to validate our emotional projections. It is better to have our feelings hurt than lose money. Find a few good sources online that cover the housing markets. Look at national homebuilder sites, real estate sites, and others for the opinions of economists. Seek out econometric models of the areas you are interested. Validate the models forecasts by looking at employment levels, population, housing supply, and home sales time on the market. It only takes a few hours to do your homework, but it takes longer to replace the money you could lose.

To end on a positive note, I hope that the book has shed some new light and sparked some new ideas on the new spectrum of real estate investment. Good luck in your endeavors.

References

Antwerp. (accessed November 23, 2009).

Bakken, Henry H. "Futures Trading - Origin, Development, and Present Economic Status." 5-7. Mimir Publishers, 1966.

Baum, Andrew. "Commercial Real Estate Investment A Strategic Approach 2nd Edition." 275-315. London: EG Books, 2009.

Black-Scholes. (accessed December 10, 2009).

Brown, Rojer J. "Private Real Estate Investment." 2-16, 19-37. San Diego: Elsevier Academic Press, 2005.

Bruges. (accessed November 30, 2009).

Commodity Market. (accessed November 19, 2009).

Commodity Money. (accessed November 20, 2009).

Damordaran, Aswath. "Investment Valuation." 88-110, 729-754. New York: John Wiley & Sons, Inc., 2002.

DiPasquale, Denise; Wheaton, William C.. "Urban Economics and Real Estate Markets." 25-34, 36-57, 150-179, 183-192, 216-235. Upper Saddle River, NJ: Prentice Hall, 1996.

Dojima Rice Exchange. (accessed December 1, 2009).

Eichholtz, Piet M; Geltner, David M, "Four Centuries of Location Value: Implications for Real Estate Capital Gain in Central Places." Limburg Institute of Financial Economics, Maastricht University, 2002.

Exchange, Chicago Mercantile. "CME Housing Futures and Options."

Fabozzi, Frank J, Christian Menn, and Svetlozar T. Rachev. "Fat-Tailed and Skewed Asset Return Distributions." 81-89,163-178, 181-194. Hoboken: John Wiley & Sons, Inc., 2005.

Fairs of Champaign. (accessed November 30, 2009).

Future Exchange. (accessed November 25, 2009).

Geltner, David, and Norman G Miller. "Commercial Real Estate Analysis and Investments." 515-546, 631-632. Mason: South-Western Publishing, 2001.

Goetzmann, William. An Introduction to Investment Theory. Yale School of Management.

History of Chicago. (accessed November 25, 2009).

History of Money. (accessed November 19, 2009).

History of the Future Exchanges. (accessed November 25, 2009).

History of Writing Ancient Numbers. (accessed November 19, 2009).

Hunt, Edwin S, and James H Murray. "History of Business in Medieval Europe 1200-1550." 212. London: Cambridge University Press, 1999.

Illinois and Michigan Canal. (accessed November 25, 2009).

JP Morgan. "CME Housing Futures: More Indications of Slowing, Even Negative, HPA." New York, 2006.

References

Kennedy, Charles R. "The Orations of Demosthenes.." 328-345. London: George Bell & Sons, 1886.

Kuhrt, Amilie. "Trade, Traders, and the Ancient City." 25-28. London: Routledge, 1998.

Matao, Miryamoto. "May/June." Journal of Japanese Trade and Industry, 1999: 39-40.

Mathers, William S. "Hedging Real Estate Development." 2009.

Mumford, Lewis. "The City in History." 441. Harcourt, Inc., 1989.

Reiss, Jonathan. "What can we learn from housing futures?" 2008.

Roehner, Bertrand. "Hidden Collective Factors in Speculative Trading." 22-27, 72-76, 119-131. Paris: Springer, 2001.

Shah, Ajay. "Black, Merton, and Scholes: Their Work and its Consequences." Economic and Political Weekly, December 1997: 3337-3342.

Spence, Donald. Futures & Options - A Guide for Traders and Investors. Chicago: Woodhead Publishing, Ltd., 1999.

Standard & Poor's. S&P/Case-Shiller Metro Area Home Price Indices. McGraw-Hill Companies, 2006.

Stock Exchange. (accessed November 20, 2009).

Syz, Juerg M. "Property Derivatives." 7-21, 35-46, 53-85. West Sussex: John Wiley & Sons Ltd., 2008.

Yu, Tony. Getting Into Property Derivatives. Investment Property Forum, 2008.

Index

affordability, 53
agricultural
  land, 10
  rent, 10
American Revolution, 34
Antwerp, 90
arbitrage, 128
average sales time, 54

Batavian Republic, 34
bid rent curve, 14
Bourse, 90
Bruges, 88
bubble, 57
bubonic plague, 24

capital value, 102
capitalization rate, 72
Chambers of Reunion, 27
Chicago Board of Trade, 93
Chicago Board Options
  Exchange, 95
Chicago Butter and Egg Board, 94
Chicago Mercantile Exchange, 94
city
  evolution, 4
clay tokens, 84
clustering, 49
commodity money, 84
commute cost, 9

comparable sales, 64
Competing Uses, 12
Computer Age, 94
correlation coefficient, 169
covariance, 188
cycles, 45

demographics, 52
Disastrous Year, 25
Dojima Rice Exchange, 92
dominant investments, 185
Dutch East India Company, 26
Dutch Republic, 20
Dutch West India Company, 21, 26

econometric model, 56
Edict of Nantes, 28
efficient frontier, 191
electronic trading, 95

fair letter, 88
Fairs of Champagne, 88
feasibility, 61
fixed leg, 121
flipping, 67, 146
floating leg, 121
forward contract, 86
future
  contract size, 126
  contract symbols, 127
  spread, 132
futures, 125

Glorious Revolution, 30
Golden Age, 20

hedge, 139
Hedging, 163
Herengracht Location Value Index, 17

income property, 71
income return, 102
industrial mix, 49

labor, 46
leverage, 62
location rent, 9
log-return, 167

mean-variance portfolio theory, 191
MPT. *See* mean variance portfolio theory

Napoleon, 34
National Council of Real Estate Investment Fiduciaries. *See* NCREIF
NCREIF, 100
net operating income, 72
net present value, 65
NPI, 99, 100

option
    American, 137
    call, 137
    European, 137
    pricing, 140
    put, 137
    strike price, 137
options, 136
    vanilla, 137
output, 46

portfolio
    diversification, 182
portfolio theory, 182
pro forma, 65
product cycle, 49
property
    value, 8
property derivatives, 96

Radar Logic Price Index (RPX), 106
real estate, 46
real estate index, 99
real estate investment trust, 197
real estate options, 136
region, 46
REIT. *See* real estate investment trust
return
    required equity, 63
Ricardian rent, 8
risk, 181
    asset, 40
    managerial, 40
    market, 41
    premium, 64

S&P / Case-Shiller Home Price Indices, 109
sales pair, 110
Sharpe ratio, 196
Sharpe-maximizing portfolio, 196
shipping contracts, 86
shock, 52
Silicon Valley, 50
speculation, 56
Stanford Industrial Park, 50
structure rent, 9
swap, 119
synthetic flipping, 146
synthetic market exposure, 145
synthetic rental property, 155

total value, 102

volatility, 183

War of the Spanish Succession, 32
Weighted Average Cost of Capital, 63

www.ingramcontent.com/pod-product-compliance
Lightning Source LLC
Chambersburg PA
CBHW031945170526
45157CB00002B/390